Desired

By The

King

Revised, Updated, and Expanded

Desired By The King

by Ruth Harvey

Sequel to:
Power Before The Throne and Reflecting The Glory

Desired By The King

Copyright © 2002
Ruth Harvey

All artwork drawn by Wade Plemons

Unless otherwise indicated, all Scripture quotations are taken from the New King James Version of the Bible.

ISBN: 978-0-9674360-6-7
Printing History: Previously released in an earlier edition under the same title, copyright 2002 by Ruth Harvey
Revised edition: 2022

FOR INFORMATION:
Please visit our web site @ www.abidingwords.com

Printed in the United States by Morris Publishing®
3212 East Highway 30
Kearney, NE 68847
1-800-650-7888
www.morrispublishing.com

Dedicated to my godly mother, Faith Edith. Mother, you have always modeled the beauty of holiness without and within. You taught me to love God by word and deed. Thank you for never compromising truth and passing it on from generation to generation.

Acknowledgments

Above all else, I exalt my Lord and Master, Jesus Christ. Each of my books is a result of Your divine enabling, for without You I can do nothing. The hungering desire of my heart is a deeper relationship with You and greater revelation into Your Word. *Therefore I love Your commandments More than gold, yes, than fine gold!* (Psalm 119:127).

My family—Steven, Angel, Miriam, and Nathan: Thank you for your constant, loving support. Next to Jesus, you are the joy and love of my life!

Dr. James Littles: Thank you for helping me hone my writing skills during my M.Div. degree program. I also appreciate your encouragement to utilize the knowledge gained during my educational journey to revise and update my books.

Renee Kleiman: My amazing niece, thank you for taking time to listen to each chapter and providing valuable feedback on this project.

Donna Ten Eyck: My longtime friend, thank you for your contribution to this project.

Wade Plemons: Artistic *'talent on loan from God'*!

Bethany Sledge: An editor, proofreader, and typesetter of excellent quality combined with an extensive knowledge of the greatest Book in the world! What more could I ask for?!!

Table of Contents

Introduction

When writing this book twenty years ago, I never envisioned the full scope of catastrophic shifts transpiring in our culture. The current full frontal attack on all longstanding civilized norms illustrates the all-out war the enemy wages against God, His creation, and divinely ordained institutions.

Who would have imagined that using conventional terminology such as male/female, man/woman, boy/girl, he/she, or him/her could be considered "hate speech" in certain situations? Now the "experts" tell us there are multiple genders, and their gender identity list continually grows as confusion reigns supreme. Yet there are only two gender reassignment surgery options available: male and female. With the inception of cancel culture, anyone who bucks this insidious trend can face job loss, forfeiture of parental rights, legal battles, school suspension, intimidation by social media mobs, verbal abuse, and even physical assault. What will the world system try to normalize next? Where does this destructive, slippery slope end? Nothing remains sacred, and the dreadful possibilities defy imagination.

Nevertheless, the foundation of God stands sure, and His Word remains unchanged despite anyone's arrogant attempt to redefine or reassign human sexuality. No, God is not confused, and we should not be confused either. Jesus' timeless response in Mark 10:6 underscores this reality, ***But from the beginning of the creation, God "made them male and female."*** The Creator Himself established the male/female identity inherent in His image bearers.[1] Indeed, humanity represents God's crowning creation. Psalm 8:4-5 declares this wondrous truth,

What are mere mortals that you should think about them, human beings that you should care for them? Yet you made them only a little lower than God and crowned them with glory and honor (NLT). God endows human beings with His glory and honor; thus, satan's transgender/transhuman agenda epitomizes his malevolent quest to usurp God's glory and honor by dehumanizing men and women.

> This invisible spiritual battle taking place in the heavenlies visibly plays out on the bloody battlefield of political correctness. Truly, it represents a coordinated satanic attack against God via His Imago Dei masterpiece. Satan wants to destroy murderously God's magnificent image altogether or else replace it with his mutilated version.[2]

Disguising himself as an angel of light, he attempts to transform humanity into his perverted image by using gender confusion, cross-hormone drugs, surgical mutilation, transhumanism, artificial intelligence, and the destruction of free will. But we are not ignorant of his devices.[3] Satan uses the same tactic repeatedly to ensnare humanity just like he ensnared Eve in Eden "by engaging in a brilliant assault that reversed God's entire orderly plan for His image bearers."[4] Sadly, instead of becoming more like God, the first parents became less of themselves. And humanity's ongoing rebellion against God's creative plan and purposes ever yields the same tragic results.

Thus, given the current situation, I believe this revision of the original content provides even greater relevancy and insight. Truly, God's Word remains a timeless source of precepts and principles, serving as an anchor during these tumultuous times. More than ever, we need to understand and to adhere to these precious truths. So, once again, the Spirit beckons us to delve deeper into God's treasure trove of hidden riches found in the secret places of His Word. Daniel 11:32-33 declares, ***The people who know their God shall be strong, and carry out great exploits. And those of the people who understand shall instruct many.*** . . . Only through divine relationship and revelation will the church become the mighty, life-giving force that destroys the death grip of demonic influence.

Desired By The King unmasks the enemy's true intentions regarding issues such as feminism, redefinition of marriage/family, cross-dressing, immodesty, and exploitation. The church must never conform to this world's fashions, fads, or belief systems. Paul admonished in Romans 12:2, ***Don't copy the behavior and customs of this world, but let God transform you into a new person by changing the way you think. Then you will learn to know God's will for you, which is good and pleasing and perfect*** (NLT, my emphasis). Isn't it interesting that the enemy adopted the term, *trans*, for his assault on God's image bearers?! He is a copycat, not a creator. God is the originator of the true *trans* agenda! He wants to *trans*form (*metamorphóō*), to change or *trans*figure each of us into a new person. Matthew and Mark used this same word to describe Jesus' transfiguration.[5] This *trans*formation refers to a divine metamorphosis; namely, in the above-quoted reference, the spiritual creative process whereby the Creator restores all that His image bearers lost in Eden. Paul described this *trans*formative process in II Corinthians 3:18, ***But we all, with unveiled face, beholding as in a mirror the glory of the Lord, are being transformed into the same image from glory to glory, just as by the Spirit of the Lord.*** The thief steals, kills, and destroys to enact his *trans*-agenda but God *trans*forms us from "glory to glory." Indeed, the church is *pro-**transformation***, and we all should support this biblical 'trans' agenda.

God invites us to become a ***transformed*** people for Him, a bride befitting the King of kings and the Lord of lords. ***So the King will greatly desire your beauty. . .*** (Psalm 45:11).

Introduction Footnotes:

1. Genesis 1:27; 5:2.

2. Ruth Harvey, *Imago Dei: Restoring the Creator's DNA* (Akron, OH: 48hrbooks.com, 2019), 38. This book offers an in-depth discussion into how men and women uniquely image God.

3. II Corinthians 2:11.

4. Harvey, *Imago Dei*, 38.

5. Matthew 17:2; Mark 9:2.

The Feminist Myth

I have often thought of myself and my friends as transitional figures, more sure of where we were coming from than where we are going. Friends of mine have described our coming of age as being on the cusp of changes that fundamentally redefined the role of women.

—Hillary Rodham Clinton

In the late 1960s, historical, unprecedented social change began rocking the moral underpinnings of American society. The cultural, social, and political tumult resulted from a prolonged assault against long-held traditional roles of men and women. Using inflammatory rhetoric, Elizabeth Cady Stanton, a notorious feminist, declared in 1869, *"The male element is a destructive force, stern, selfish, aggrandizing, loving war, conquest, acquisition, breeding . . . discord, disorder, disease, and death."* Ironically, as the feminist aggression unfolded through the past centuries, the very traits disdained as masculine deficiencies characterized the movement.

As women ran headlong down the pathway of female domination, their defiance left a wake of devastation. They broke every rule in the "good girl" handbook, defying sanctions against abortion, single motherhood, divorce, and unmarried cohabitation. The following statistics reveal some of the tragic long-term consequences of these unwise choices:

◆ Since 1970, the proportion of traditional families– Mom, Dad, and their 2.2 biological kids–has decreased by 35 percent.

◆ There are more households composed of people living alone or childless couples than households of married parents living with children.

◆ After 1980, the number of couples choosing to live together rather than marry climbed 80 percent. The greatest increase is among couples over thirty-five, many of those people previously divorced. One in four Americans over eighteen today has never married. In 1970, it was one in six.[1]

A Washington Post article, entitled "Less than half of U.S. kids now have a 'traditional' family," illustrates the far-reaching catastrophic consequences of our convoluted culture. Christopher Ingraham writes, "As of 2013, only 46 percent of U.S. kids live in a traditional family structure of two parents in their first marriage. An additional 15 percent live with a parent who has been remarried at least once, 34 percent live with a single parent, and 5 percent have no parent at home—this latter group is most likely living with a grandparent, according to Pew Research Center. By contrast, 73 percent of American kids lived with a traditional family back in 1960."[2] Researchers generally agree "that children of unmarried parents tend to have a tougher time in life: more poverty, more instability, and more problems at school, among other things."[3] This aftermath of ruin begs the question, What really is the devastating force in our society: the acceptance of conventional male/female roles or the destruction of those roles?

Decrying the male species as "stern" and "selfish," the feminists seemingly took on these unfavorable attributes but in a greater degree than imagined at the outset of this insurrection.

The Feminist Myth

Shouting obnoxiously into the microphone during their gatherings, they boldly declared, "We're fierce, we're feminists, and we're in your face!" Comparing the definition of "stern" versus "fierce" highlights the deterioration of the female species in their quest for domination. *Fierce*, meaning "brutal, bloodthirsty, ferocious, murderous, savage, barbarous," denotes a far more destructive connotation than *stern*, which means "harsh, cruel, unfeeling, and adamant." The statement, "We're in your face!" underscored radical feminists' disregard for anyone else's thought or the effect of their actions on subsequent generations.

Determined to prevail no matter the cost, militant feminists ran roughshod over anyone who stood in their way. The drumbeat of their propaganda gradually conditioned society to allow full-scale murder of innocents in the womb at any stage of pregnancy, all in the name of convenience. David Kupelian observes, "In one of the most successful marketing campaigns in modern political history, the 'abortion rights' movement—with all its emotionally compelling catchphrases and powerful political slogans—has succeeded in turning what once was a crime into a fiercely defended constitutional right."[4] Media personalities, slick politicians, celebrities, and influencers pontificate about women's control over their own bodies and contend that abortion represents a personal choice between a woman and her doctor. After all, the right to choose represents a basic American right. Using the term, *fetus*, conveys the concept of "an ugly, non-human, disposable lump of tissue" so physicians violate their consciences under the manipulative guise of "helping women."[5]

With the advent of social media, the videos of abortion advocates celebrating by literally dancing on the graves of their helpless victims in an act of grotesque desecration are quite disturbing. The blood of millions of the unborn saturates feminism's pro-choice altar as proponents literally scream on video, "We love killing babies." This sort of dark rhetoric reveals the demonic roots of this evil agenda.

During the revision of this book, California is trying to pass Assembly Bill 2223 to legalize infanticide of abortion survivors even up to twenty-eight days after birth, and Maryland wants to follow suit. Thus, abortion advocacy continues its horrific slide down the bloody, slippery slope of legalized murder of the most vulnerable victims even though "barely 25 percent of Americans embrace unfettered abortion on demand."[6] Yet this radical and murderous agenda remains in effect. Some of the responses to California AB 2223 reveal alarming callousness towards the murder of innocents. One young woman gave her opinion in an interview, "Yeah, whatever helps women achieve their dreams and however that happens helps all of us." Another responder said he supports the bill and thinks that infanticide should be optional for mothers for up to a month after birth. Other interviewees voiced their approval of the bill using foul language to mock the murder victims and said they would have multiple abortions until they are ready to parent.

Kupelian rightly observes, "In truth, millions of people who think of themselves as pro-choice are victims of sophisticated marketing campaigns designed to appeal to their deepest feelings about freedom and equality while simultaneously hooking them through powerful appeals to their selfishness."[7] The *fierce* reality of abortion's "sheer barbarism and brutality" essentially "amounts to infant torture and murder" all in the name of selfish convenience.[8]

This ongoing massacre results from modern entitlement culture's embrace of the illusion of unrestrained sexual freedom without consequences. Abandoning reasonable self-restraint, many indulge their lustful cravings as the persistent assault against the institution of marriage and family continues. Feminist ideology belittles stay-at-home moms as non-contributing members of society and deems climbing the corporate ladder as life's most fulfilling choice. Professor Vivian Gornick declared, "Being a housewife is an illegitimate profession . . . the choice to serve and be protected and plan towards being a family-maker is a choice that shouldn't be. The heart of radical feminism is to change that."[9] Moreover, the feminist community encourages women not to seek any kind of male assistance, and they characterize matrimony as bondage and rape. Radical feminist author, Andrea Dworkin, equated marriage with prostitution and labeled it an extremely dangerous and oppressive institution for women. Robin Morgan, an editor at *Ms.* magazine, stated, "We can't destroy the inequities between men and women until we destroy marriage."[10] Gloria Steinem, a prominent modern-day feminist, also viewed marriage as captivity and advocated to abolish and reform the institution of marriage. She famously said, "By the year 2000, we will, I hope, raise our children to believe in human potential, not God. . . . We must understand what we are attempting is a revolution, not a public relations movement."

Divorce reform represents another destructive ideological weapon advocated by the nineteenth-century feminists Elizabeth Cady Stanton and Ernestine Rose. The continued pursuance of this reformation, however, bore bitter fruit in the succeeding generations. In 1920, the *Atlantic Monthly* magazine stated, "The riot of divorce has become almost an orgy."

◆ By 1922, there were 131 divorces for every 1000 marriages. The rate rose steadily afterward until the 1960s, when it skyrocketed, hitting 50 percent in the 1970s and remaining there ever since.

◆ California passed the first no-fault divorce law in 1920. Most states followed. Alimony has been drastically limited, half of all divorced mothers with custody of their children receive no child support, and many more fathers win custody of their children. Some experts blame "the feminization of poverty" on the new divorce laws and attitudes. One study found that a man's living standard generally rose 42 percent after a divorce; conversely, the standard of living for his ex-wife and children fell by 73 percent.

♦ The term *displaced homemakers*, coined in the 1970s, describes women with no job skills outside the home who find themselves cast out of economic security after divorce. In 1990, there were 16 million such women in America, three out of five living below the poverty level. The motto of the Displaced Homemakers Network, a Washington, DC, service agency, is, "Just a man away from poverty."[11]

Considering the preceding statistics, have women benefited from divorce reform? Has this feminist agenda item made their lot in life better or worse? Stephen Baskerville, a political science professor at Howard University, notes that fatherlessness remains the single greatest factor underlying violent crime, substance abuse, unwed pregnancy, suicide, and the gang culture, among other negative outcomes. Further, unrestrained divorce represents big business in both the private and public sector. It constitutes a judicial cash cow that lines the pockets of "judges, lawyers, psychotherapists, mediators, counselors, social workers, child support agents, and others. The divorce revolution has spawned a public-private industrial complex of legal, social service and psychotherapeutic professionals devoted to the problems of children, and especially children in single-parent homes. Many are women with feminist leanings."[12] No matter their pious platitudes regarding the plight of these children, Baskerville says, "The fact remains that these practitioners have a vested interest in creating as many such children as possible. The way to do it is to remove the fathers."[13] Eliminating fathers enables the state to function as protector and provider while also creating multiple problems requiring solutions; thus, uncontrolled divorce becomes "a marvelous tool" facilitating "infinite expansion of government power."[14]

The Feminist Myth

Interestingly, Vladimir Lenin, in one of his first acts, enacted no-fault divorce statutes to facilitate and further the 1917 communist revolution. Celebrated Soviet expert Mikhail Heller relates that both Lenin and Stalin deemed it necessary to destroy and restructure the family in order "to maintain control of the people. This statute, along with the communist encouragement of sexual immorality during marriage, approval of abortion, and forcing women out of the home into the workforce, accomplished its purpose of destroying the Russian family."[15] Given the unrelenting attempts to strip our freedoms and turn America into a socialist/communist country, a similar playbook appears to be in use. Under the guise of liberation, a tyrannical jackboot is crushing the hard-won freedoms of "we the people."

Continuing our examination of the feminist myth, the picture of reality shines through when we juxtapose their denunciations with their actions. Pointing an accusatory finger, Elizabeth Cady Stanton said men were "aggrandizing, loving war, conquest, acquisition." Yet some of the main feminist objectives contain these very components. Flouting convention in the name of sexual equality and self-expression, feminists embraced militant action. At the onset of the twentieth century, militant suffrage activity in England spurred American suffragists further in their quest for control. Their tactics included violence, riots, and arson. Mary Heaton Vorse praised the violence of British suffragettes: "I cannot imagine anything that would affect better the moral health of any country than something that would blast the greatest number of that indecent, immoral institution—the perfect lady—out of doors and set them smashing and rioting."[16] They preposterously presumed that women's abandoning their homes and destroying everything standing in the way of their quest for "freedom" would somehow better our nation.

The sexual revolution represents another outgrowth of the eradication of feminine restraints. For decades, even centuries, women were protected, chaperones were commonplace at social events, and courtship took place under the watchful eyes

21

of a girl's parents. Even amid nineteenth-century decorum, however, perversion existed, and lesbianism flourished within the woman's suffrage movement. Touting same-sex relationships as a viable alternative lifestyle, radical feminist author Jill Johnson viewed men as the enemy and contended that true political revolution was not possible until all women were lesbians.[17] This perverse lifestyle gained momentum as militant women increasingly abandoned their God-ordained role of womanhood.

During the Roaring Twenties, the flapper—young, hedonistic, sexual—became a symbol of the age with her bobbed hair, rouged checks, and shorter skirts. This "new" woman danced, smoked, and flaunted her sexuality before her elders. The sensuality of the flappers signaled a powerful behavioral and ideological change in American culture. Coeducational state universities flourished and created a setting in which young men and women broke away from past constraints of sexual propriety. "Are we as bad as we're painted?" asked a young woman at the Ohio State University. "We are. We do all the things our mothers, fathers, aunts, and uncles do not sanction, and we do them knowingly."[18]

During the 1930s, the Great Depression seemed to sober the nation for a while, but with the onset of World War II, the theme of sexual liberation emerged. The intensity of wartime emotion contributed to short-term affairs and loose morality. Finally, the 1960s ushered in a total breach of the moral barricade as youth experimented with new frontiers of sexual freedom. The downward spiral into sensual degeneration continues at an alarming rate, destroying everything in its path. Just think, this momentous cultural shift started with tiny seeds of inflammatory rhetoric against God's pattern for the human family!

The greatest price has been extracted from our offspring as boys and girls are battered, abused, and destroyed by live-in relationships. Sexually transmitted diseases remain at an all-time high. Abortion on demand consumes more innocent lives than any prior human holocaust. Strangers raise our children in daycare centers. "Babies" are having babies! Latchkey kids come home to empty houses, having as a result immature minds and hearts filled with violent anger. Many of these find satisfaction in constructing bombs and planning murderous shooting sprees. While they seek acceptance and love by engaging in promiscuous activity or criminality within the gang community, the seeds of sedition continue to bring forth a bitter harvest. Violent crime pervades our communities as mobs riot, smash storefronts, loot, burn businesses, and murder in cold blood. *Discord, disorder, disease, and death* have become a way of life. Hmm. . . . I thought those destructive characteristics were destined for eradication once women achieved their goal of liberated feminism.

Anger and stress rage in our society now more than ever, producing a greater demand for therapists, counselors, and Prozac. Why? Because it remains impossible to go contrary to the divine design and ever achieve true freedom. The following essay illustrates the beauty of God's blueprint as He created the first man and woman.

God's Message to Women

When I created the heavens and the earth, I spoke them into being. When I created man, I formed him and breathed life into his nostrils. But you, woman, I fashioned after I breathed the breath of life into man because your nostrils were too delicate. I allowed a deep sleep to come over him so I could patiently fashion you. Man was put to sleep so he could not interfere with My creativity.

From one bone I fashioned you, and I chose the bone that protects man's life. I chose the rib, which protects his heart and lungs and supports him as you are meant to do. Around this one bone, I shaped and modeled you.

I created you perfectly and beautifully. Your characteristics are as the rib, strong yet delicate and fragile. You provide protection for the most delicate organ in man, his heart. His heart is the center of his being; his lungs hold the breath of life. The rib cage will allow itself to be broken before it will allow damage to the heart. You were not taken from his feet to be under him, nor were you taken from his head to be above him. You were taken from his side to be held close as you stand beside him.

I caressed your face in your deepest sleep. I held your heart close to Mine. Adam walked with Me in the cool of the day and yet he was lonely. He could not see or touch Me but could only feel My presence. So I fashioned in you everything I wanted Adam to share and experience with Me: My holiness, My strength, My purity, My love, My protection and support. You are special because you are an extension of Me.

So, Man, treat woman well. Love and respect her, for she is delicate yet strong. In hurting her, you hurt Me. In crushing her, you only damage your own heart. Woman, support and work together with the man as I designed you to do. In humility, show him the power of emotion I placed within you. In gentle quietness show your strength. In love, show him that you are the rib that protects his inner self.

—Author Unknown

From the beginning, the Creator encoded His DNA into His image bearers, and every human comes into the world with the Imago Dei engraved on his/her body, soul, and spirit. Moreover, God's inaugural words about humanity in Genesis 1:26-28 destroy the notion of men having greater value than women.[19] Unfortunately, the further humanity moves from God, the less people understand themselves, resulting in massive gender confusion. The scope of this work does not allow for an exhaustive exploration into how men and women image God, but a brief overview based on the material in my book, *Imago Dei: Restoring the Creator's DNA*, will provide some important insight to the topic at hand.[20] Humanity images God collectively, but each gender uniquely images Him as well. Given the biblical prevalence of male pronouns and imagery for God, many envision Him as male and believe the female bears the divine image to a lesser degree. Stephen Boyd wisely observes, "Because we have split human qualities into polarized masculine and feminine characteristics, and projected only one sex onto God, we have a stunted sense of God's fullness."[21] We are created in His image and not the other way around! God reveals His image in women as well as men but through different aspects. Moreover, the complete revelation of His image necessitates the inclusion of both male and female; otherwise, the divinely complex portrait remains incomplete.

Reading Scripture through a Western lens and projecting our cultural male/female norms onto God's Word often distorts it and limits our ability to understand the rich layers of meaning therein. God is neither a man nor a woman; nevertheless, the Bible's use of masculine/feminine imagery for the Divine remains foundational for understanding humanity's identity as God's image bearers and its influence upon the human experience. Indeed, God endowed each gender with a portion of His attributes and thereby provided the basis for human gender distinctions. Therefore, God constitutes the foundation for the distinctively male and female dimensions of human existence. Consequently, humanity does not define God; rather, God defines humanity! Gilbert Bilezikian avers, "Femaleness pertains to the image of God as fully as maleness. God is neither male nor female since He is neither a physical nor a sexual being. He transcends both genders as they are both comprehended within his being."[22][23]

Men and women differ in appearance and actions, have different strengths and different value systems, and use different strategies in their life approach. In short: men are preoccupied with things, theories, and power; women are more concerned with people, morality, and relationship.[24] Moreover, these gender differences reflect divine attributes invested within women and men and reveal the contours of His divine image. Men reflect God's powerful, protective, rational, judicious, problem-solving nature; women reflect His personal, relational, emotional, nurturing, compassionate character. Of course, humanity's imaging function reflects but in no way limits the richness and complexity of our Creator.[25] Equal in worth, yet wonderfully distinctive in gender giftings, men and women, by God's design, interrelate in a complementary way.

Scripture affirms the creation of two sexually distinct human beings as inherently good.[26] To be male is good and to be female is good! Gretchen Gaebelein Hull states, "It cannot be emphasized enough that only after the creation of *both* sexes do we read in Genesis 1:31: 'God saw all that He had made, and it was very good.' Man alone was not good. Man and woman together were very good."[27] Carolyn Custis James notes, "God laid out his game plan in Genesis" and He strategically assembled the relational male/female team to carry out the mission.[28] He created men and women to live in close fellowship, to complete each other socially, and to help each other vocationally in fulfilling their mutual responsibility of ruling the earth (Genesis 1:26).[29]

Sadly, the devastation of the Fall brought division between God's image bearers and launched the age-old battle of the sexes inherent in the feminist agenda. What is the ultimate intent of feminism? Is it the result of a group of innocent women suffering from oppression and poor self-esteem? Beyond a doubt, female nineteenth-century leaders like Susan B. Anthony established a variety of important reform movements including abolition, temperance, missionary, and benevolent associations, and their quest for inclusion in the political process represented a very legitimate objective.[30] In the grand scheme, however, did a much deadlier motive lie behind this entire movement?

Perhaps the following citations from feminist Naomi Goldenburg shed light on the enemy's true agenda masquerading behind the facade of valid concerns spawned by the rotten fruit of sexism.

> All feminists are making the world less and less like the one described in the Bible and are thus helping to lessen the influence of Christ on humanity. "God is going to change," I thought. "We women are going to bring an end to God. As we take positions in government, in medicine, in law, in business, in the arts and finally in religion, we will be the end of Him. We will change the world so much that He won't fit in anymore."
>
> The feminist movement in Western culture is engaged in the slow execution of Christ and Yahweh. Yet very few of the women and men now working for sexual equality within Christianity and Judaism realize the extent of their heresy.

Nothing makes this truth clearer than the feminists' current stance regarding the transgender movement and its assault on all things female. Under the guise of gender inclusivity, some groups have replaced words like *women* and *mothers* with denigrating terms such as *birthing persons* or *pregnant people*. During a recent Supreme Court confirmation hearing, the nominee, who was nominated because she was a woman, refused to even define the term, *woman*, when questioned by Senator Marsha Blackburn. Judge Jackson said she was not a biologist and therefore could not answer this basic question. Apparently, you are not qualified to define basic terms unless you have some sort of degree. What convoluted reasoning! The simple question, "What is a woman?" is now verboten, and even medical professionals refuse to answer it definitively. Yet men who identify as women are called "transgender women," and now, after centuries to the contrary, some absurdly claim that men can get pregnant. Talk about fake news!

In a further twist of ludicrous irony, the 2022 "Woman of the Year," who was also nominated as the first "female" four-star admiral in the United States Public Health Service Commissioned Corps, is really a biological man. And the top "female" swimmer recently nominated for the NCAA Woman of the Year award by the University of Pennsylvania is also a biological male! Under the transgender banner, men who cannot make the grade in a man's world and male competitions can now identify as women, crash women's sports, and take their medals and scholarships. Biological men shoving women out of the way, cutting in line, and robbing them of their feminine achievements appear to be the transgender version of "male chauvinism." Yet the feminist influencers utter nary a peep of protest. Crickets! If the advancement of women represented the true purpose of feminism, why the deafening silence as the dismantling of everything they supposedly worked for continues before all our eyes?

And so everything comes full circle as men dominate women but this time in a much more perverted, sinister manner. Delano Squires, a guest on Tucker Carlson's show, gave one of the best explanations of how 'woke' women have basically "woken" themselves into irrelevance. Contending that transgenderism represents one of the biggest threats to civilization, Squires said, "God made male and female, and whether you believe in Genesis or genetics, that is what everyone has believed basically up until seven years ago." He explained that some of the most powerful women in media, journalism, politics, and business aided and abetted this entire transgender movement. These same women spent their entire careers bemoaning their difficulties achieving equality, but they have allowed themselves to be cowed into silence by a large group of activists and a small group of men with serious mental health challenges. Squires points out the irony of these women's finally finding a group of men they are willing to submit to because when Rachel

Levine and Lia Thomas, who are both biological males, speak, they remain silent. "So, in effect, they are about to diversity and equity themselves right out of existence." Ironically, this woke agenda represents another form of the patriarchy that all feminists supposedly decry, one that essentially robs women and girls of equal opportunities while completely undermining their six-decade-long message. Squires concluded by claiming the feminists have essentially gone from saying, "I am woman; hear me roar," to singing, "This is a man's world." Men posing as women kick the chair out from under them and take their seats at the table. Thus, the aggressive erasure of women continues.

Yet again, the lie dating to the genesis of civilization entrapped humankind. *In the day you eat of it your eyes will be opened, and you will be like God, knowing good and evil.*[31] Eve loitered around the tree, and the serpent convinced her that her life lacked fulfillment unless she partook of the forbidden fruit. Similarly, he used the same argument to entice modern women to sample the same tree. Nevertheless, while professing to exalt women, feminism instead does the exact opposite because it is rooted in misogyny, the *hatred* of women. Under the guise of "advancement for women," it really seeks to nullify them by destroying their feminine role. Indeed, this is feminism's fundamental flaw. Feminism identifies male goals and methods as the ideal for women. According to Anne Moir and David Jessel, "It denies the sexual difference, denies the very essence and thus the very value, of the feminine."[32] Megan Fox concurs, "Today's feminists do nothing but harm women at every turn"; look at the issues they support—abortion on demand, casual sex, free birth control, and pornography.[33] She continues, "Nothing about their platform is freedom for women. Everything about it puts women under men, literally, while excusing men from any responsibility."[34]

Do not fall for the feminist fallacy that equality with men literally means to become like men. Men and women are not interchangeable. If a cooking pot and a crystal vase decided to trade places, the vase would crack under the heat while the pot would do a poor job of enhancing a floral bouquet. In the same manner, humanity cannot go against the Creator's divine design and expect to succeed. The law of the Lord remains perfect and irrefutable despite any gainsaying oratory. Therein lies the utter insanity and irony of the feminist myth!

Chapter One Footnotes:

1. Louise Bernikow, *The American Women's Almanac* (New York, NY: Berkley Publishing Group, 1997), 313.

2. Christopher Ingraham, "Less than half of U.S. kids now have a 'traditional' family," washingtonpost.com, 12/23/14 https://www.washingtonpost.com/news/wonk/ wp/2014/12/23/less-than-half-of-u-s-kids-now-have-a-traditional family/

3. Ibid.

4. David Kupelian, *The Marketing of Evil: How Radicals, Elitists, and Pseudo-Experts Sell Us Corruption Disguised as Freedom* (Nashville, TN: Cumberland House Publishers, 2005), 189.

5. Ibid., 206.

6. Ibid., 113.

7. Ibid., 208.

8. Ibid., 205.

9. Ibid., 112.

10. Robin Morgan, *Sisterhood is Powerful* (New York: Random House, 1970), 537.

11. Bernikow, *The American Women's Almanac*, 306-7.

12. Stephen Baskerville, Ph.D., "Divorce as Revolution," http://www.ejfi.org/family/family-26.htm

13. Ibid.

14. Ibid.

15. Mikhail Heller, *Cogs in the Wheel* (New York: Knopf, 1988), 168-179, cited in Charles E. Corry, "Evolution of Society," http://www.ejfi.org/Civilization/Civilization-2.htm

16. Sarah M. Evans, *Born for Liberty* (New York: Simon & Schuster, 1989, 1997), 168.

17. Kupelian, *The Marketing of Evil*, 112.

18. Evans, *Born for Liberty*, 177.

19. Carolyn Custis James, *Half the Church: Recapturing God's Global Vision for Women* (Grand Rapids: Zondervan, 2011), 50.

20. See my book, *Imago Dei: Restoring the Creator's DNA*, for an in-depth look into how men and women image God.

21. Stephen B. Boyd, *The Men We Long to Be: Beyond Domination to a New Christian*

Understanding of Manhood (New York: HarperCollins, 1995), 118.

22. Gilbert Bilezikian, *Beyond Sex Roles: What the Bible Says about a Woman's Place in Church and Family, 3rd edition* (Grand Rapids: Baker Academic, 2006), 18-19.

23. David Norris, "Anthropology" (Class lecture notes, Systematic Theology, UGST, October 28, 2014).

24. Carol Gilligan, *In a Different Voice* (Cambridge: Harvard University Press, 1993), 97.

25. Gretchen Gaebelein Hull, *Equal to Serve: Women and Men Working Together Revealing the Gospel* (Grand Rapids: Baker Books, 1998), 156.

26. Linda L. Belleville, *Women Leaders and the Church: Three Crucial Questions* (Grand Rapids: Baker Books, 2000), 98.

27. Hull, *Equal to Serve*, 155, emphasis original.

28. James, *Half the Church*, 139.

29. Hull, *Equal to Serve*, 155.

30. Evans, *Born for Liberty*, n.p.

31. Genesis 3:5.

32. Anne Moir and David Jessel, *Brain Sex: The real difference between Men and Women* (London: Wise Owl Secrets Publishing, 2015 Kindle edition), 174.

33. Megan Fox, "9 Secrets to Keep Your Daughter from Becoming a Slut," pjmedia.com 3/9/14, https://pjmedia.com/lifestyle/2014/3/9/9-secrets-to-keep-your-daughter-from-becoming-a-slut/

34. Ibid.

Identity Crisis

My husband is trying to decide if he's comfortable with the person I've become. I'm not a passive "Yes honey, anything you want" kind of woman. The only way men of our generation are going to change is if we keep changing ourselves. I told him, "If you say, 'Stay at point A, don't go to point B,' I'm immediately going to point B." He has to understand that my goal is to keep going: B, C, D, E, F. If he wants to come along, fine, but I can't be dragged back. I'm a woman and I'm growing.

—Anonymous[1]

The preceding statement embodies the ongoing conflict between the sexes resulting from the devastation of the Fall. With one lethal blow, the Fall's devastation toppled the dual towers [God/humans, male/female] of strategic relationship, causing perpetual relational fallout in a broken world.[2] As explained by Gilbert Bilezikian, "Adam's life became subject to the ground from which he was taken, and Eve's to the man from whom she had been taken. The ruler-subject relationship between Adam and Eve began after the fall."[3] Carolyn Custis James sums up the resultant relational male/female brokenness, "Instead of ruling and subduing the earth, they turned against each other and sought to rule and subdue each other."[4] Male domination and female subordination do not exemplify God's ideal. Instead, these dysfunctional consequences of the Fall prove the need for the redemption of both men and women.[5]

Unfortunately, dysfunctional confusion reigns supreme as humanity continues to cast aside and trample underfoot the

Creator's master blueprint for men and women. Indeed, the feminist revolution continues to feed the beast of male/female relational dysfunction as evidenced by ever-increasing gender confusion and role reversal. David Kupelian rightly observes, "The bending and sometimes breaking of traditional gender roles permeates our society in obvious and subtle ways. Popular culture promotes sexual confusion at every turn."[6] In a study of the demise of morals, marriage, and family, a convergence of several factors emerges that interconnects the outward appearance and actions with the inward attitudes. Indeed, the outside reflects the inside! Jesus gave this principle in Mark 7:20-23,

> *It is what comes from inside that defiles you. For from within, out of a person's heart, come evil thoughts, sexual immorality, theft, murder, adultery, greed, wickedness, deceit, lustful desires, envy, slander, pride, and foolishness. All these vile things come from within; they are what defile you* (NLT).

To better understand our arrival at this point in history, we need to examine the correlation between cross-dressing and its effects on gender confusion, role reversal, and the destructive dismantling of sexual norms. Author George Gilder explains in his classic book, *Men and Marriage*, "To the sexual liberal, gender is a cage. Behind cruel bars of custom and tradition, men and women for centuries have looked longingly across forbidden spaces at one another and yearned to be free of sexual roles."[7] Establishing a new set of values and beliefs about male/female behavior required a societal redefinition of long-standing gender symbols associated with what it means to be a man or a woman.[8] Claudia Brush Kidwell and Valerie Steele write, "Our beliefs about how men and women should look are part of a powerful, complex, and pervading system of values about what is appropriate male and female behavior."[9] Accordingly, challenging of gender symbols linked with a change in appearance represents a "symbolic precursor to social change."[10]

In America, skirts, trousers, and hair represent some of the most prevalent gender symbols. Thus, the effort to effect sweeping social change commenced by challenging the fundamental appearance of men and women in these key areas. Today, both men and women wear trousers, but women fought for that right. Even now "wearing the pants" equates to "acting like a man." Why do we associate trousers with masculinity and skirts with femininity? The following quote illustrates how the history of a garment influences our perception.

> *In all times and places men and women have worn distinctively different clothing or adornment. The meanings given to clothes are influenced by the history of a garment. In cultures where trousers have become symbols of masculinity, women wearing trousers causes questions about women looking and acting like men. If appearance is a sign of identity, what does it mean when women lift weights and wear trousers while men largely reject the sartorial symbols of femininity?*
>
> —Robert J. Steinberg

In their quest for equality, early feminists promoted the right to dress like men as one of their leading objectives. They understood that changes in attire would facilitate their larger aim of changing gender conventions by removing a biblical worldview and lessening the influence of Christianity. Thus, the outward symbolism of wearing masculine apparel gave voice to their true intentions of dismantling biblical prohibitions against cross-dressing so it would be considered normative and widely accepted by the general populace. The acts of Amelia Bloomer, a leading mid-nineteenth century feminist, exemplified this inborn intention. By proposing in her publication, *The Lily*, that women wear a trousered outfit, Mrs. Bloomer contradicted the long-held belief that natural law dictates the attire of men and women. This idea sparked intense criticism across the country because it blurred the visual lines between the sexes. Her opponents believed that adopting symbols from the opposite sex would threaten societal norms and lead to radical changes in male/female relationships.

An engraving of Mrs. Bloomer wearing the controversial trousered outfit appeared in the September 1851 edition of *The Lily.* Bloomer jokingly wrote that she hoped her appearance would not shock her female readers, and her male readers would not mistake her for a man. Elizabeth Cady Stanton, another celebrated feminist of that time period, attended a women's rights convention in 1852 wearing a similar trousered ensemble. One journalist accused Mrs. Stanton of dressing like a man down to boots, pants, a dickey, and a vest.

Detractors of Bloomer's trousered ensemble expressed their concern that women who dressed in this manner might start to behave like men as well as look like them. When young men began wearing long hair almost a century after the Bloomer costume question, the same concerns over gender symbolism arose. The long-haired "choir boy" Beatles and the "bad boy" prancing, pouting Mick Jagger with his long hair, skintight jeans, eyeliner, and dangling earrings helped to feminize the culture.[11] Long hair on men and men's apparel worn by women "challenged the accepted appearance of men and women in fundamental ways."[12] Many believed the blurring of gender lines would disrupt society's equilibrium and possibly lead to societal destruction.[13] Sadly, those fears were not unfounded.

The revolutionary social change sweeping current culture feels akin to careening down a life-threatening, slippery slope of extreme gender chaos, but these radical deviations did not transpire overnight. The feminization of men/boys and the masculinization of women/girls required a long process of dismantling centuries-long gender norms through the introduction of subtle changes that gradually devastated the natural order. At first, the changes sparked outrage, but society eventually caved to growing pressure to cast aside gender distinctives. Each concession led to greater moral decay, slowly eroding the foundations of fundamental, biological norms. David Kupelian notes, "Today, after decades of progressive destruction of traditional standards, the sexual mores that once formed the foundation of Western civilization have pretty much been reduced to rubble, on top of which has been erected a secular, sophisticated but extraordinarily sexualized culture."[14] The insane push to normalize transgenderism now bombards us, and any attempt to push against this cultural psychosis meets savage resistance.[15]

In 2013, California led the way down this slippery slope as the first state in the United States that required public schools to let transgender students use bathrooms and play on sports teams corresponding to their personal gender identities. The Minnesota State High School League followed suit in 2014 and overwhelmingly approved the participation of transgender students in female sports in its five hundred public schools.[16] Consequently, in fall 2015, transgender male students competing in female sports gained full access to women's locker rooms with a permission slip from parents, guardians, or health care professionals.[17] In 2015, Ontario, Canada, adopted sex education curriculum that introduced eighth graders to six different genders and four sexual orientation options.[18] Currently, the Biden administration and the DOE seek to amend Title IX and force all schools to let transgender males compete in female sports, use female locker rooms and bathrooms, and sleep in the same rooms on school-sponsored trips. Any schools refusing to comply with these insane orders can lose their federal funding.

These dangerous policies cause irreparable damage and open the door for even greater moral collapse. The unthinkable continues to happen! Schools plan field trips to drag queen shows, essentially homosexual strip clubs. A July 5, 2022, news item reports that Washington state school board director, Jenn Mason, told KTTH radio host, Jason Rantz, she plans to teach a sexual 'pleasure' class to nine-year-olds at her local sex shop. Drag queens host children's story hours in libraries. Teachers sexually prey on their students. Instead of teaching reading, writing, and arithmetic, school curriculum promotes gender dysphoria as staff members facilitate gender transition surgeries without parental knowledge or consent. New York City Mayor, Eric Adams, tweeted out support of these dangerous policies on June 16, 2022: "Drag storytellers, and the libraries and schools that support them, are advancing a love of diversity, personal expression, and literacy that is core to what our city embraces."

Under the banner of inclusivity, the blatant grooming of innocent children transpires sometimes at the hands of their own parents. How did we end up in such a deadly moral quagmire? Well, the enemy, ever the subtle serpent, understood acceptance of this sort of perversion required the same tactic successfully used in Eden. Convince humanity of the inferiority of the Creator's design for His image bearers and get them to bite into the fruit of rebellion. Initiate the protracted process of deathly self-destruction with one small bite of poisoned fruit until their rebellion against the Creator eventually brings deathly ruin.

In Romans 1:24-27, the apostle Paul described the tragic result of humanity's rebellion against the Creator.

> *So God said, in effect, "If that's what you want, that's what you get." It wasn't long before they were living in a pigpen, smeared with filth, filthy inside and out. And all this because they traded the true God for a fake god, and worshiped the god they made instead of the God who made them—the God we bless, the God who blesses us. Oh, yes!*
> *Worse followed. Refusing to know God, they soon didn't know how to be human either—*

women didn't know how to be women, men didn't know how to be men. Sexually confused, they abused and defiled one another, women with women, men with men—all lust, no love. And then they paid for it, oh, how they paid for it—emptied of God and love, godless and loveless wretches (*The Message*).

What an apt description of our culture! Evil forces seek to redefine what it means to be human and what it means to be male or female by replacing it with a twisted non-binary entity that bears no resemblance to the Creator's image. Civilization remains in crisis, namely an *identity crisis*. For ages, a person simply identified him/herself by name. Now, people state their preferred pronouns, and woe be to the person who forgets, for that one will be penalized. Kupelian asks how we arrived here. "Women were being 'liberated'—or so we were assured—from 'bondage' to their traditional roles, and thereby enabled to develop themselves personally, professionally, and spiritually as never before. Men were also supposedly 'freed' to express their more sensitive, nurturing, feminine side. In this fuzzy utopian fantasy, society was supposed to evolve into a great big happy androgynous paradise where everyone is equal to everyone else in every way."[19] Instead, children get punished and suspended from school for referring to a fellow student according to his/her biological, God-given sex instead of the classmate's preferred pronouns, "they and them."[20]

The moral deterioration continues as some even claim to identify as animals and birds! Romans 1:28-32 chronicles the wretched outcome of this rebellion:

Since they thought it foolish to acknowledge God, he abandoned them to their foolish thinking and let them do things that should never be done. Their lives became full of every kind of wickedness, sin, greed, hate, envy, murder, quarreling, deception, malicious behavior, and gossip. They are backstabbers, haters of God, insolent, proud, and boastful. They invent new ways of sinning, and they disobey their parents. They refuse to understand, break their promises, are heartless, and have no mercy. They know God's justice requires that those who do these things deserve to die, yet they do them anyway. Worse yet, they encourage others to do them, too (NLT).

Truly, confusion reigns supreme as the world descends into madness!

The February 2002 edition of *Reader's Digest* featured a very interesting article, "Are Boys Really the Weaker Sex?" The same feature appeared in an earlier issue of *U.S. News & World Report*. The article states:

Boys are in serious trouble. They get the lowest grades that teachers dole out. They make up two-thirds of students labeled learning disabled. They are the suspects in eight out of ten arrests on drug and alcohol charges and are arrested for over 70 percent of juvenile crimes. They are also less likely to go to college. By 2007, universities are projected to enroll 6.9 million men compared with 9.2 million women.

These college enrollment statistics continue to hold true almost twenty years later. According to the National Student Clearinghouse Research Center, women comprise nearly 60 percent of enrollment in universities and colleges, and men reach just over 40 percent. "Fifty years ago, the gender proportions were reversed."[21] The remainder of the aforementioned *Reader's Digest* feature set forth various rationales as to the possible reasons for such a major malfunction among the younger male generation. But the article never articulated the true underlying reason for the masculine emotional problems; it stems from the convolution of male/female roles.

"Today's politically correct culture labels traditional male behaviors such as risk-taking, achievement, and love for adventure as 'toxic masculinity.' The American Psychological Association's newly released guidelines for men and boys assert that traditional masculinity negatively influences their mental health."[22] Professionals classify common boy behavior, such as difficulty paying attention, fidgeting, running, climbing, procrastinating, and blurting out answers, as clinical symptoms of ADHD. They "eagerly diagnose them as suffering from a mental illness and put them on drugs" such as Ritalin despite disturbing evidence of untimely deaths and harmful effects to the heart connected to such drugs.[23] Kupelian rightly assails this trend as he states, "Labeling millions of children with ADHD and drugging them to make their behavior more acceptable is nothing short of a national scandal."[24]

The feminist movement decried men in general to such an extent the entire male psyche remains under constant attack. If a man compliments a woman, it is often labeled as sexual harassment. Gentlemanly conduct such as opening doors, giving up a seat, offering a helping hand, or paying for a meal can be met with hostility. Affirmative action demands the hiring of women and minorities even if a man has better qualifications for the job. Rewritten history books depict men such as Christopher Columbus and George Washington as evil white men. Yet maverick feminist Camille Paglia courageously reminded her men-hating colleagues that masculinity remains "the most creative cultural force in history."[25] Feminist-inspired experts want to destroy masculinity, a force that for millennia "tamed the wilderness, constructed civilizations, revolutionized life with dazzling inventions, and sacrificed its own life to protect women and children, so they can construct a new version."[26] Ironically, feminists disparage men while they seek to become like them and dress like them.

God, in His awesome foresight and knowledge, understood the serious issues at stake and addressed the integral issue of cross-dressing in His Word. Under various laws of morality, Moses included this principle in Deuteronomy 22:5, *A woman shall not wear anything that pertains to a man, nor shall a man put on a woman's garment, for all who do so are an abomination to the LORD your God.* Jason S. DeRouchie states, "On the surface the prohibition relates to what the APA terms 'gender expression'—'the way a person acts to communicate gender in a given culture' through things like dress. At a deeper level, however, the law assumes a more fundamental rule—that there are two biological sexes—male and female—and that what is gender normative in God's world is that one's biological sex should govern both one's gender identity and expression."[27] God framed these prohibitions using the Hebrew durative sense, meaning the word "not" should be read as "never": "A woman shall *never* wear a man's garment, nor shall a man *ever* put on a woman's cloak."[28] DeRouchie affirms, "From God's perspective, there is never a permissible time for the type of cross-dressing addressed in this passage."[29]

"Everyone wore robes back in the Bible days" remains one of the main arguments set forth by opponents of this particular principle. Nevertheless, the Word of God contains clues that indicate a distinction in the attire of males and females. The restrictive term used in Deuteronomy 22:5 for woman's 'cloak' (*simlāh*) specifically refers to an outer garment or wrapper only worn by women.[30] DeRouchie says the contrasting term used for the man's 'garment' (*kelî*) reflects a broader meaning encompassing male clothing, ornaments, vessels, or equipment including weapons of war.[31] Certain styles of dress, ornaments, and items differentiated men and women within the Israelite culture.[32] Therefore, this injunction highlights the need to guard against gender confusion by aligning gender expression with one's biological sex.

DeRouchie also notes that Deuteronomy 22:5 uses the word *geber* for man instead of the more common *'ish* because the latter often means husband when paralleled with woman but "*geber* never does in any of its twenty-four OT uses."[33] The use of *geber* reflects the importance of this law for the broader society. He avers, "*From God's perspective maleness and femaleness bears implications beyond the home or gathered worshipping community. It also impacts daily life in society.*"[34]

The succeeding passages of Scripture provide further evidence of this gender differentiation: ***Then the hand of the LORD came upon Elijah; and he girded up his loins and ran ahead of Ahab to the entrance of Jezreel*** (I Kings 18:46). The NKJV footnote for "girded" says "Tucked the skirts of his robe in his belt in preparation for quick travel."

Then he said to Gehazi, Get yourself ready, and take my staff in your hand, and be on your way. If you meet anyone, do not greet him; and if anyone greets you, do not answer him; but lay my staff on the face of the child (II Kings 4:29). The NKJV footnote says "Get yourself ready" literally means "Gird up your loins." The skirt of the robe was wrapped around the legs and tucked in the belt to gain freedom of movement.

And Elisha the prophet called one of the sons of the prophets, and said to him, "Get yourself ready, take this flask of oil in your hand, and go to Ramoth Gilead (II Kings 9:1). Again, the NKJV footnote explains "Get yourself ready" means "Gird up your loins."

Now prepare yourself like a man; I will question you, and you shall answer Me (Job 38:3; 40:7). In the NKJV footnotes, the phrase "prepare yourself like a man" in both verses literally means to "gird up your loins like a man." These verses use *geber*, the broader term for man, as does Deuteronomy 22:5.

Thou therefore gird up thy loins, and arise, and speak unto them all that I command thee: be not dismayed at their

faces, lest I confound thee before them (Jeremiah 1:17, KJV). The terminology "to gird up the loins or prepare yourself like a man" pertains to a distinct male action in response to his manly duties such as fighting, farming, running, and working. To avoid getting tangled up in his garment, an active man tucked his robe into his waistband, creating a trouser-like effect. It is interesting to note how God told Job to face Him in a masculine posture as exhibited by Job's attire. Similarly, God commanded Jeremiah to array himself in manly garb prior to his prophesying. The evolution of men's trousers quite possibly came about from the earlier practice of men "girding up their loins."

Further contemplation of Deuteronomy 22:5 reveals an even deeper understanding concerning this important injunction. Firstly, God established that *A woman shall not wear anything that pertains to a man*. The word *pertains* means "to have reference to, to belong as an adjunct, or accessory." Simply put, this verse says women should not cross-dress in clothing that belongs to a man, refers to, or characterizes masculine apparel. This negates the argument, "I do not wear men's clothing. I am wearing women's slacks." As noted prior, historical evidence irrefutably establishes trousers in all forms as men's apparel. In their book, *Women in Pants*, Catherine Smith and Cynthia Greig acknowledge the fact that women wearing this sort of male raiment is cross-dressing that plays with gender identity. They write, "Sometimes mistaken for men, modern women who wore trousers blurred the gender lines, often to assert their sexual interest in women as well as overtly express their equality with men."[35] From the beginning, God created men and women as equals, but equality does not equal identical!

Furthermore, the New Testament also addresses the issue of proper female attire. Paul wrote in I Timothy 2:9-10, *In like manner also, that the women adorn themselves in modest apparel, with propriety and moderation, not with braided hair or gold or pearls or costly clothing, but, which is proper for women professing godliness, with good works*. The Greek word for *apparel*, καταστολή, means "a garment let down" referring to a long, flowing robe-like garment, dress, or attire.[36] This word describes the sort of modest apparel appropriate for godly Christian women. The New Testament never uses this word for men's attire; it only uses this description for women's apparel.[37]

The next portion of Deuteronomy 22:5 reads, ***nor shall a man put on a woman's garment***. In 1970, avant-garde designer, Rudi Gernreich, predicted that men and women would wear skirts and trousers interchangeably. After the 1960s' cultural shift, he thought pants and skirts would lose their significance as gender symbols. However, his prediction did not come to pass and probably never will. "It took more than a century for women to wear pants in public; and few modern men have made skirts a part of their wardrobe."[38] There never has been and never will be a big market for feminine attire for men. Every normal, red-blooded man I know would never be caught dead in a dress or a skirt. Male cross-dressers must shop in the women's department to fulfill their deviant fantasies.

From the outset, our Creator understood the female desire to push the boundaries of gender distinctives as well as the overwhelming male rejection of wearing feminine attire. The feminist agenda and its systematic attack on gender distinctives did not surprise God. He knew satan would use this tactic as a calculated entry point to wage war on His image bearers and lead them down the path of destruction. Consequently, these verses, Deuteronomy 22:5 and I Timothy 2:9-10, reveal His marvelous foreknowledge. Moreover, His Word is written in a manner applicable to every age, generation, and culture.

According to Deuteronomy 22:5, cross-dressing represents an abomination unto the Lord, and this sort of abomination remains the same in both Testaments. Abominations to humankind may change, but abominations to God, such as human sacrifice, homosexuality, idolatry, witchcraft, dishonest gain, and innocent bloodshed, never change.[39] Jason DeRouchie elucidates that "idolatry gives glory to someone other than YHWH;

witchcraft looks to means other than God's word to discern his will" or foretell the future, and "dishonest gain diminishes the value of God's image in others."[40] In the same way, trans-genderism and gender confusion distort God's nature invested in His image bearers. It "maligns humanity's ability to reflect, resemble, and represent God rightly in this world."[41]

In its original context, Deuteronomy 22:5 provides guidance for maintaining "divinely-created biological and gender distinctions within the community" to cultivate an environment that properly images God and displays His supremacy.[42] Unfortunately, the modern evangelical community succumbed to cultural pressure, and most mainline churches abandoned biblical gender distinctives in the last few decades. A bite of the poisoned fruit of compromise eventually blurred the lines of holy separation until behaviors and practices once considered sinful are now deemed normative in many denominations. Christians became like the world instead of changing it. For example, most Evangelicals view female cross-dressing as normative and consider the biblical prohibition against this habit as outdated and irrelevant. Consequently, countless Christian women who profess their earnest love for God and sincere devotion to His Word cross-dress without any compunction, whether wittingly or unwittingly. On the other hand, how would these people feel if men, especially Christian men, engaged in cross-dressing?

An article, entitled "Bending Gender," appeared in the June 16, 2002, edition of *WORLD* magazine (a Christian-based weekly news publication). The editorial vocalized the outrage of the denominational Christian world in response to trans-vestites who cross-dress. In response to the article, my friend, Esther Henry, wrote a brilliant rejoinder which follows:

Dear WORLD Editor:

As a missionary living overseas, we get the magazine very late sometimes, and then by the time all of them arrive, we have some "catching up" to do. We always look forward to your wonderful magazine and read it cover to cover!

I am writing this letter in response to an article in your June 16 issue, "Bending Gender" under the Education section. I couldn't help but read it with amusement, although I'm sure most who read about Warfield/Rivers' blatant cross-dressing were appalled.

May I briefly point out the reason for my amusement: evangelical Christianity as a whole (of which we are also a part) seems so shocked by the cross-dressing of men. Why should they be? Women all over Europe and America and other developed nations of the world have been cross-dressing for nearly [110 years] (and now they're doing it in almost every undeveloped nation as well). Women will cut their hair (many times as short or shorter than a man's), they wear trousers and jeans on a consistent basis, they work the jobs that were only reserved for men just a few decades ago, etc. The list goes on.

Christian women have been following the world's way of cross-dressing for years. Why, then, should Christianity be so shocked when a man follows suit? If it's not a sin for a woman to cross-dress, then why would it be a sin for a man? Just something for all of us in Christendom to think about. . . .

Esther Henry
Missionary's wife to Papua New Guinea

P.S. I write this letter with "tongue in cheek," because [our organization teaches] very strongly the separation of the sexes, although we are labeled "too strict" by the rest of Christianity. They would never allow their men to cross-dress, yet they "label" us for teaching our women not to—It doesn't make any sense.

As the previous letter points out, the *identity crisis* gripping our nation infiltrated and deceptively influenced most of the Christian world as well as secular society. It certainly begs the question, "If the Christian community had maintained biblical gender distinctives and not caved to cultural pressure, could the tide of gender confusion have been stemmed?" Regrettably, instead of going against the tide, the majority went with the flow. Consequently, the church world is sliding down the same slippery slope of destructive social revolution in this post-modern era. By way of example: On March 22, 2022, Duke Divinity School hosted a 'pride' service in Goodson Chapel, where students proclaimed God's acceptance and support of LGBTQ relationships. Using Genesis 32:22-31 as a text, an M.Div. student defended gender transition as biblical. The students invoked God's name in dangerously perverse ways tantamount to blasphemy.[43] This twisted version of Scripture results from denominations and church leaders' affirming and explaining sin instead of confronting it by speaking the truth in love. God's love does not rejoice in iniquity; it rejoices in truth.[44]

Many mainline churches display rainbow flags and embrace cultural/religious dualism as formerly prohibited behaviors, including sexual perversion, are not only tolerated but also widely accepted and considered culturally correct. This dangerous trend leads to the exaltation of culture above the Word of God; however, we cannot consciously or unconsciously allow culture to dictate or influence our theology. Also, important to note: God's covenant rainbow has seven colors—red, orange, yellow, green, blue, indigo, purple—while the pride symbol has only six. Seven represents God's number for completeness or perfection, but Revelation 13:18 says six is the number of a man, namely the beast. There is a reason the pride flag has only six colors—it represents the enemy's perversion of God's plan, His perfection, and His covenant promise.

Isn't it interesting that this celebration of perversion invokes the term, *pride*, as its moniker? God's Word warns against pride and contains countless verses detailing His abhorrence and resistance to it. Pride and iniquity corrupted Lucifer, causing him to be expelled from heaven.[45] Proverbs 16:18 declares, "Pride goes before destruction," and I Peter 5:5 states, "God resists the proud." Yet the churches that cave to cultural depravity often invoke the phrase, "God is still speaking," to validate their acceptance and celebration of perverse behaviors. Nevertheless, Malachi 3:6 declares, "For I am the LORD, I do not change." Hebrews 13:8 echoes the divine principle, "Jesus Christ is the same yesterday, today, and forever." Of course, God still speaks, but He does not contradict His forever settled Word. Therefore, we must ask, "Do we have ears to hear what the Spirit is saying?"

In Matthew 5:13-16, Jesus called us to be the salt of the earth, a preserving agent that stops corruption. ***But what good is salt if it has lost its flavor? Can you make it salty again? It will be thrown out and trampled underfoot as worthless*** (NLT). Jesus also commissioned His disciples to be the light of the world, to stand out in the darkness like a shining city on a hill and not to blend in or hide our identity under the basket of cultural conformity. ***Instead, a lamp is placed on a stand, where it gives light to everyone in the house*** (NLT). Sadly, a majority of Christians blend in instead of standing out. To be salt and light in the world is not a religious catchphrase or catchy song lyric—it represents our sacred duty as God's holy people.

Throughout the centuries, however, humankind has struggled with many misconceptions concerning the issue of holiness. There are those who try to achieve holiness by living a monastic life of solitude. Others endured daily scourging and slept on stone floors while some refrain from using modern appliances, power machines, or technical devices. History records that Simon Stylites, a Syrian Christian ascetic, tried to achieve holiness by living thirty-seven years on a small platform on top of a pillar near Aleppo. His food was hoisted to him, and vermin fell off his body only to be caught by the people below who came to share in his 'holiness.' Defining holiness by human imperfections instead of by God's perfection produces some bizarre behaviors. Consequently, many define holiness as a set of manmade, legalistic rules. They view the beauty of holiness from a negative perspective, calling it bondage instead of seeing its real identity of liberty in Christ Jesus. Thus, people fall prey to false teaching that promises freedom but produces bondage. Second Peter 2:20 says they end up entangled and enslaved by worldly pollutions once again.

So what is the proper definition of holiness? Firstly, only God can truly define holiness since it originates from Him. Without God, there is no holiness! The Hebrew word for *holy*, *Qodesh*, means set-apartness, sacredness, separateness. The Greek word for *holy*, ἅγιος (transliterated *Hagios*) means a sacred object of awe. It also carries the idea of physical purity, blameless morality, and ceremonial consecration; however, most scholars accept the general meaning of separateness. Thus, separateness defines one of the most important elements of God's holiness. He is holy because He is separate. God's absolute virtue exemplifies a vital part of His separateness; thus, holiness remains associated with moral purity. Moreover, God's purity represents the positive perfection of His character, not simply the negative absence of defilement and sin. In Exodus 15:11, Moses also connected God's holiness with His awesome glory and superiority, *Who is like You, O LORD, among the gods? Who is like You, glorious in holiness, Fearful in praises, doing wonders*? No god compares to Him!

Furthermore, God remains unique in the fact that He is the only One Who *is being* (see Hebrews 11:6) while everyone else 'has being.' Acts 17:28 says we derive our 'being' from Him. In like manner, God is the only One Who is Holy; therefore, we obtain our holiness through Him. Holiness is not something we achieve; it is something we receive! We find in II Peter 1:3-4 that God enables us to live a godly life and to escape the world's lustful corruption through the impartation of His divine power, and we become partakers of the divine nature. According to Romans 1:4, God's Spirit, which we receive, is the Spirit of holiness or the Spirit of separation unto God. The Holy Spirit remains the divine enabler, the supreme source of holiness guiding us into a separated lifestyle because holiness and separation remain inseparable! Consequently, I Peter 1:15-16 commands, *But as He who called you is holy, you also be holy in all your conduct, because it is written, "Be holy, for I am holy."* We are set apart because we are holy, not the other way around. Living a holy life is the outward evidence of an inward work of salvation—after the Holy Ghost has come upon us!

As a holy people, we should embrace the doctrine of separation and strive to live in accordance with the standards set forth in God's Word. We need to understand, however, that biblical standards and personal convictions are not the same. Too many people equate their personal convictions with biblical standards and then turn into the judge and the jury, casting judgment on everyone else. Personal convictions are just that—they are personal! Maintain your personal consecrations and do them unto the Lord, but do not turn them into a measuring rod used to beat others up. On the other hand, biblical standards are just that—they are biblical! These principles set forth in God's Word represent divine directives meant to facilitate our spiritual growth. Ephesians 4:13-15 identifies this process as maturing in the Lord and *measuring up to the full and complete standard of Christ. Then we will no longer be immature like children. We won't be tossed and blown about by every wind of new teaching. We will not be influenced when people try to trick us with lies so clever they sound like the truth. Instead, we will speak the truth in love, growing in every way more and more like Christ, who is the head of his body, the church* (NLT). Becoming more like Jesus remains the end goal of this spiritual maturity process.

So let us consider the doctrine of separation within its biblical context. The doctrine of separation represents the oldest doctrine in the Bible and permeates the entire Creation account. God made a separation with His first words and first act: He divided light from darkness (Genesis 1:3-5). He separated them, named them, and gave them a distinct role to play. This separation set the pattern for every other creative and redemptive work of God. Having separated and defined the difference between light and darkness, God next made a distinction between the water of the atmosphere and the water of the sea (Genesis 1:6-8). In His ongoing work of pulling order from chaos, God next made further separation and distinction between land and sea (Genesis 1:9-10).

This theme persists throughout the Creation narrative as God continued His work of separation on the fourth, fifth, and sixth days. Then, at the apex of His creativity, God created man and woman, two sexually distinct human beings uniquely endowed with His image. Moreover, He created them equal: equal in their relationship to Him, equal in their call to rule over the world, equal in their responsibility to image God in unique but complementary ways, equal in their dependence on Him to fulfill their mission.[46] Thus, at the end of the creative week, what started out as a mess—without form, with no distinction, confused in darkness and chaos—was now neatly in order. There was light, order, boundaries, separation, and distinction, which included male/female gender. Everyone and everything had a purpose. This opening chapter in the glorious story of redemption reveals the defining characteristics of God's redemptive work. When God is at work, He brings order through separation and distinction.

Indeed, the establishment of separation and order reflects His essential character of holiness. In the Garden of Eden, God commanded Adam and Eve not to partake of the tree of knowledge of good and evil. He instructed them to separate themselves from this source of evil knowledge. God called Abraham to leave Ur of the Chaldees, and he had to separate himself from his country and kindred. The Exodus narrative pulsates with the concept of separation as God declared in Exodus 8:23, *I will make a clear distinction between my people and your people.*

Moreover, when the Israelites exited Egypt, they engaged in the ultimate act of separation. God's creative and redemptive work always involves separation and distinction. It remains at the core of redemption's story.

Likewise, II Corinthians 6:17-18 declares, *"Come out from among them And be separate," says the Lord. "Do not touch what is unclean, And I will receive you."*
"I will be a Father to you, And you shall be My sons and daughters," Says the LORD Almighty.

This passage of Scripture reveals the key to correcting the exploding *identity crisis* and bringing order out of the gender chaos. First Peter 4:17 says this course correction begins at the house of God. It's time for the church to turn on the light instead of cursing the darkness. Forsake worldliness with its systematic corruption and compromise. Embrace the biblical doctrine of separation. Receive God's holiness. Affirm male/female gender differences in every aspect of behavior, dress, and lifestyle as a celebration of God's image and creation.

Jason DeRouchie rightly observes, "Gender identity and gender expression is about God's glory and about maintaining God-created distinctions on earth that in turn point to the ultimate distinction of God and His bride."[47] Our Creator used this redemptive principle in Genesis 1—He restored order to the chaos through separation and distinction. It worked then and it still works today.

Chapter Two Footnotes:

1. Susan B. Evans, Ed.D., and Joan P. Avis, Ph.D. *The Women Who Broke all the Rules* (Naperville, IL: Sourcebooks, Inc. 1999), 147.

2. Harvey, *Imago Dei*, 25.

3. Bilezikian, *Beyond Sex Roles*, 42.

4. James, *Half the Church*, 141.

5. Harvey, *Imago Dei*, 25-26.

6. David Kupelian, *How Evil Works: Understanding and Overcoming the Destructive Forces That Are Transforming America* (New York, NY: Simon & Schuster, 2010), 174.

7. George Gilder, *Men and Marriage* (Gretna, LA: Pelican, 1986), 115.

8. Claudia Brush Kidwell and Valerie Steele, *Men and Women: Dressing the Part* (Washington: Smithsonian Institute Press, 1989), 146.

9. Ibid., 144.

10. Ibid.

11. Kupelian, *How Evil Works*, 174.

12. Kidwell and Steele, *Men and Women*, 146.

13. Ibid.

14. Kupelian, *How Evil Works*, 176.

15. See Dr. Quentin Van Meter's lecture, "The Terrible Fraud of Transgender Medicine" for more information on this topic: https://www.youtube.com/watch?v=uC0zn0D_MyM

16. Jason S. DeRouchie, "Confronting the Transgender Storm: New Covenant Reflections on Deuteronomy

22:5," *JBMW* 21/1 2016: 59.

17. Ibid., 60.

18. Ibid., 59.

19. Kupelian, *How Evil Works*, 171.

20. Joshua Arnold, "Using 'Wrong' Pronouns Could Lead to Suspensions in Virginia Public Schools," dailysignal.com, 5/16/22, https://www.dailysignal.com/2022/05/16/using-wrong-pronouns-could-lead-to-school-suspensions-in-virginia-public-schools/

21. Charlotte West, "An unnoticed result of the decline of men in college: It's harder for women to get in," hechingerreport.org, 10/27/21, https://hechingerreport.org/an-unnoticed-result-of-the-decline-of-men-in-college-its-harder-for-women-to-get-in/

22. Harvey, *Imago Dei*, 68.

23. Kupelian, *How Evil Works*, 166.

24. Ibid., 167.

25. Camille Paglia, "It's a Jungle Out There," *Newsday*, 1991, https://archive.seattletimes.com/archive/?date=19910217&slug=1266788

26. Kupelian, *How Evil Works*, 174.

27. DeRouchie, "Confronting the Transgender Storm," 62.

28. Ibid., 63.

29. Ibid.

30. Ibid.

31. Ibid.

32. Ibid.

33. Ibid.

34. Ibid., italics original.

35. Catherine Smith and Cynthia Greig, *Women in Pants: Manly Maidens, Cowgirls, and Other Renegades* (New York, NY: Harry N. Abrams Publishers, 2003), 103.

36. Daniel Segraves, "Old Testament Law & the New Testament," (Class lecture notes, Old Testament Foundations, October 23, 2013).

37. Ibid.

38. Kidwell and Steele, *Men and Women*, Plate 11.

39. See Deuteronomy 12:31; Leviticus 18:22; 20:13; Deuteronomy 7:25-26; 13:12-18; 27:15; 17:1; 18:9-14; 25:13-16; Proverbs 11:1; 20:23; 6:16-19.

40. DeRouchie, "Confronting the Transgender Storm," 64.

41. Ibid.

42. Ibid., 65.

43. Hope Rawlson, " 'God is Queer,' Duke Divinity Students Proclaim," juicyecumenism.com 4/5/22, https://juicyecumenism.com/2022/04/05/queer-god-duke-divinity/

44. I Corinthians 13:6.

45. Ezekiel 28:14-19.

46. DeRouchie, "Confronting the Transgender Storm," 64.

47. Ibid.

The Spirit of Jezebel

But there was no one like Ahab who sold himself to do wickedness in the sight of the LORD, because Jezebel his wife stirred him up (I Kings 21:25).

Jezebel, the Phoenician wife of King Ahab, embodies a biblical proverb to God's people, and her name remains a byword for everything considered abominable in His eyes. First and Second Kings recount her story, which began with her union to Ahab, king of Israel. Each time the Scripture emphasizes Ahab's sin, it mentions Jezebel's influence in the same breath. The saga of King Ahab's reign commences in I Kings 16:29 and fills the remaining portion of the book. He received more literary space in the Old Testament than any other king of Israel or Judah. Lawrence Richards notes, "This is due to the significant religious struggle that developed during his reign."[1] Immediately following his introduction, I Kings 16:30 says Ahab's evil in the Lord's sight exceeded the evil of all of Israel's previous kings.

This champion of evil followed the wicked example of Jeroboam by paying homage to the two golden calves set up in Bethel and Dan. Then, his sinful lifestyle degenerated to a new level of idolatry when he married Jezebel, daughter of Ethbaal of Tyre, king of the Phoenicians, a group of Semites descended from the Canaanites.[2] Janet Howe Gaines writes, "Phoenicia consisted of a loose confederation of city-states, including the

61

sophisticated maritime trade centers of Tyre and Sidon on the Mediterranean coast."[2] Sidon was deemed a center of vice and idolatry. The Phoenicians worshiped a variety of gods and goddesses; however, Baal, the Canaanite fertility and agricultural god, represented their chief deity. Josephus said Ethbaal served as a priest of Astarte before he violently displaced his brother, Phelles, and seized the throne.[3] Astarte, also known as Asherah or Ashtoreth, remained the primary Phoenician goddess, a goddess of fertility, love, and war, often linked with Baal.[4] Janet Gaines notes that as the king's daughter, Jezebel possibly served as a priestess during her formative years but "in any case, she was certainly raised to honor the deities of her native land."[5]

After marrying Ahab, Jezebel moved to Jezreel, a city that served the Lord. Unfortunately, Israel continually struggled with forsaking Yahweh and worshiping false gods. Thomas Cahill says the Canaanite fertility cults compromised the pure worship of Yahweh, evidenced by the discovery of ancient inscriptions "dating to the period of the monarchy that seem to be prayers to 'YHWH and his Asherah.' "[6] God's people fell prey to "a kind of paganizing syncretism" when they "settled down to the business of farming and herding among their Canaanite neighbors."[7] Zephaniah 1:4-5 references Israel's religious dualism that combined the worship of Yahweh with obeisance to the hosts of heaven on their rooftops. In the daily fight for survival, the Israelites often gave in to the temptation of engaging in cultic fertility rites to increase their productivity.

Jezebel, however, established idolatry on a grander scale in Ahab's court. Her tables fed 450 prophets of Baal and 400 of the Astarte prophets of the grove while she ordered the slaughter of Jehovah's prophets. According to Brenner, Jezebel's extensive patronage of these pagan prophets shows she retained "her own compound within the royal court" with "an independent administrative organization" that she financed and controlled.[8] Ahab abdicated his duty to administer religious affairs and let Jezebel use her vast resources to embed Baal worship in Israel.[9]

The Spirit of Jezebel

Jezebel easily induced Ahab into Baal worship since it revolved around worshiping a calf, reminiscent of Jeroboam's two golden calves. *Baal* means "owner or husband" in Hebrew. As a result, when Ahab introduced the worship of Baal-Malqart, the owner or lord of Tyre and Sidon, into Israel, he openly rejected Yahweh as owner and Lord of Israel.[10] Ahab's idolatrous actions and profane insolence provoked the Lord's anger to a greater degree than ever.[11] Canaanite religion included every conceivable vice, such as snake worship, male and female prostitution, child murder, and sacrifice. Baal's priests and prophets murdered countless little children in sacrifice to their god.[12] Sound familiar? It seems that evil spirit remains alive and well, and it feeds at abortion's bloody altar of child sacrifice.

To better understand the saga of Ahab and Jezebel, let us briefly examine some of the myths and practices associated with Baal worship. Known as the god of sky and rain, Baal, son of Dagon, had a consort named Anath (also known as Asherah at Samaria in the ninth century BC).[13] Baal and Anath had three daughters: Talliya, goddess of dew, Padriya, goddess of clouds, and Arsiya, goddess of the earth.[14] As both goddess of war and goddess of love and sensuality, Anath's slaughterhouse tactics against the opponents of Baal, her fellow deity, are detailed:

Anath swells her liver with laughter
Her heart is filled with joy
For in Anath's hand is victory
For knee-deep she plunges in the blood of soldiers
Neck-high in the gore of troops
Until she is sated.[15]

This slaughter resulted in fertility for the land:

She draws water and washes
With dew of heaven
Fat of earth.[16]

Baal worship included human sacrifice as previously noted, as well as self-torture, kissing the image, and grotesque fertility rites with male/female temple prostitutes in the idolatrous groves. Soon beautiful temples dedicated to Baal worship dotted Israel's landscape. When the prophets of God opposed Jezebel's idolatry, she ordered their execution as the queen became the first female religious persecutor in biblical history. She so effectively injected the poison of idolatry into Israel's veins that the entire nation suffered from God's judgment.

God sent the prophet Elijah to King Ahab with a message of doom against disobedient Israel. *As surely as the LORD, the God of Israel, lives—the God I serve—there will be no dew or rain during the next few years until I give the word!* (NLT) With a stroke of divine irony, God mocked Baal's power since his adherents believed he controlled the rain and produced abundant crops. Yahweh revealed His supremacy over the false god of sky and rain in a manner reminiscent of His conquest over Egypt's gods during His showdown with Pharaoh.

After Elijah delivered the prophecy, God told him to go east and hide by Kerith Brook, near its entry into the Jordan River. While the relentless sun blistered the countryside, drying up the creeks and rivers, Elijah hid in the Kerith canyon on the other side of the Jordan. The man of God enjoyed miraculous sustenance as ravens brought bread and meat every morning and evening. God instituted the first successful food delivery service long before Grubhub, Uber Eats, or DoorDash came into existence. Amazingly, He changed the nature of ravenous birds and used them to feed His prophet. By contrast, transforming the temperament of rebellious Queen Jezebel remained impossible as she doubled down in committing atrocities.

When the brook dried up, God directed Elijah to a new place of provision, the city of Zarephath in Sidon, because He had already prepared a widow to feed him. Walking to the city gates, the weary prophet saw a lone woman gathering firewood. He asked her:

"Please, would you bring me a little water in a jug? I need a drink." As she went to get it, he called out, "And while you're at it, would you bring me something to eat?" She said, "I swear, as surely as your GOD lives, I don't have so much as a biscuit. I have a handful of flour in a jar and a little oil in a bottle; you found me scratching together just enough firewood to make a last meal for my son and me. After we eat it, we'll die." Elijah said to her, "Don't worry about a thing. Go ahead and do what you've said. But first make a small biscuit for me and bring it back here. Then go ahead and make a meal from what's left for you and your son. This is the word of the GOD of Israel: 'The jar of flour will not run out and the bottle of oil will not become empty before GOD sends rain on the land and ends this drought.' "[17]

Now the widow faced two choices: would she heed the request of the man of God and do as he asked or harden her heart and refuse? The decision would determine the destiny of her and her son. Many thoughts probably raced through her mind as she considered her meager supplies and pondered the prophet's pledge of provision. Choosing to obey Elijah's request, the woman returned home and prepared the prophet's meal. And the word of the Lord came true—the flour bin never ran out and the jar of oil never dried up throughout the time of need. God provided daily food for her and her family as well as Elijah during the famine. Gerard Van Groningen notes, "This Phoenician woman, in whose land Baal was honored as the god of fertility, the sun, and the owner of all nature, learns that the Lord, whom Elijah serves, alone supplies food and drink."[18]

Her decision also yielded an unforeseen benefit. Because the widow chose to take care of the man of God, he was present when her son died and she most needed the prophet. Elijah took the boy upstairs to his room, laid him on the bed, and fervently prayed for divine intervention. God heard his petition and resurrected the widow's son. Thus, Elijah also taught the widow "that the Lord who sustains life is the Lord of life."[19]

Jesus referenced this episode in Luke 4:25-26, *Certainly there were many needy widows in Israel in Elijah's time, when the heavens were closed for three and a half years, and a severe famine devastated the land. Yet Elijah was not sent to any of them. He was sent instead to a foreigner—a widow of Zarephath in the land of Sidon* (NLT). Even though Israel had many widows, did God send His prophet outside its borders because the spirit of Jezebel had pervaded the land? Instead of sustaining the prophets, Jezebel slew the prophets. Evidently not one Israelite widow would have heeded Elijah's request since the queen's murderous influence permeated Israel. Ironically, the Lord sent His prophet to Sidon, Jezebel's own hometown.

The spirit of Jezebel despises true men and women of God and seeks to destroy them. Be careful not to fall under its evil influence by undermining and injuring spiritual authority. This sort of deadly attack only results in your own destruction and that of your family. Please do not kill the prophets, the men and women of God in your life. Instead, learn a lesson from the widow by nurturing a healthy relationship with the godly leaders who care for your soul. Then, when life happens and tragedy strikes, the needed prayer support will be there so God can do miracles on your behalf and breathe life into your situation.

After three and one-half years of drought, the time for a spiritual showdown arrived. Summoning all Israel and Jezebel's idolatrous minions to Mount Carmel, Elijah challenged the people: *How long are you going to sit on the fence? If GOD is the real God, follow him; if it's Baal, follow him. Make up your minds!* (*The Message*)

When the people remained silent, he set forth the rules of the confrontation. It was one anointed prophet of God against

850 false prophets of Baal. Each side must make a sacrifice, and the true God would answer by fire.

Agreeing to the contest, Baal's prophets built their altar. After laying their slain bullock on the altar, they started calling on their god. As the hours passed, the heavens remained silent, so the frenzied worshipers frantically leapt upon the altar. Still nothing happened. About noon, Elijah mocked their foolish efforts. *"You'll have to shout louder," he scoffed, "for surely he is a god! Perhaps he is daydreaming, or maybe he's relieving himself. Or maybe he is away on a trip or is asleep and needs to be wakened!"* (NLT)

Crying all the louder, they cut themselves according to their custom with knives and swords until the blood gushed out on them. They raved all afternoon, using every religious trick and strategy in the book but to no avail. Finally, at the time of the evening sacrifice, Elijah called the people together and repaired the broken-down altar of the Lord. Building it out of twelve stones in remembrance of the tribes of Israel, he made a trench around the altar. Laying the wood in order and cutting the bullock in pieces, Elijah told the people to pour twelve barrels of water over the waiting sacrifice. The purpose of pouring out the water seems twofold. Firstly, given the famine and scarcity of water, it represented an extreme sacrifice to the Lord. Secondly, since water quenches fire, it served to validate further the power of the one true and living God.

Standing before the sodden altar, Elijah prayed a simple prayer, *"LORD God of Abraham, Isaac, and Israel, let it be known this day that You are God in Israel and I am Your servant, and that I have done all these things at Your word. Hear me, O LORD, hear me, that this people may know that You are the LORD God, and that You have turned their hearts back to You again."* Immediately the fire of the Lord fell from heaven and consumed everything the prophet had prepared—the sacrifice, the wood, the stones, and the dust—and it licked up the water in the trench.

When all the people saw it, they fell on their faces and cried, *The LORD, he is the God; the LORD, he is the God* (KJV).

Reveling in God's glorious display of power, Elijah singlehandedly slew all 850 prophets of Baal and Astarte. The human "conflict between Ahab and Jezebel" mirrors the divine "conflict between Yahweh and Baal."[20] After the destruction of Jezebel's idolatrous influence, Elijah prayed earnestly until the heavens opened, and thirst-quenching waters rained upon the parched ground. James 5:17-18 references this incident, *Elijah was a man with a nature like ours, and he prayed earnestly that it would not rain; and it did not rain on the land for three years and six months. And he prayed again, and the heaven gave rain, and the earth produced its fruit.* American theologian Craig Keener says, "The miracle of securing rain eventually came to be viewed as equivalent to raising the dead."[21] When Ahab told Jezebel about the events, however, she arose in fury and sent a life-threatening message to Elijah, *So let the gods do to me, and more also, if I do not make your life as the life of one of [my prophets] by tomorrow about this time.*

Instantly, Elijah's fear and flight nature kicked in, and he turned to run for his life. Elijah's response was not due to cowardice or depression but a keen recognition of Jezebel's authority and motivation to carry out her threat.[22] A cave in Horeb became his hideout in similar fashion to Obadiah's hiding God's prophets in a cave. Just think, this powerful prophet confronted an entire nation, 850 false prophets, and a wicked king. Yet one fierce woman who controlled the kingdom sent him running for his life. Her intimidating threat made him forget the contest on Carmel and God's magnificent display of power. It took several days for Elijah to recover from his fear of Jezebel and venture back into ministry. God had to send an angel, a strong wind, a fire, and an earthquake. Finally, a still, small voice summoned him out of his hiding place and sent him back into service.

The spirit of Jezebel intimidates, manipulates, and assassinates, and the story of Naboth's vineyard recorded in I Kings

21 provides further illustration of this spirit's malevolent nature. Set against the backdrop of mythology surrounding Baal worship, the vineyard incident reveals amazing similarities between Jezebel and her patron goddess, Anath, also known as Asherah.

Ancient lore tells of Baal's attempt to coerce Anath into convincing her father, El, to give him a palace. No favor or request from Baal seemed too much for Anath to honor. She told Baal that he needed only to ask, and she would deliver. Then, she reminded him of her past achievements.

> *Have I not crushed Yamm, El's darling?*
> *Nor annihilated the great god, River?*
> *Have I not muzzled the dragon*
> *Nor crushed the crooked serpent*
> *Mighty monster of seven heads?*[23]

At the conclusion of the narrative, Anath appeared before El and demanded that he honor Baal's request for a palace. She threatened El with violence if he did not grant the request. El, extremely frightened by his own daughter's threats, hid from her in his own house![24] Recall this Canaanite myth and Anath's actions as we examine the account of Naboth's vineyard.

First Kings 21 commences with an attempted real estate transaction on the part of King Ahab. He espied Naboth's vineyard, which lay just beyond the palace precinct, and the king wanted it as a vegetable garden. Naboth, however, utterly refused the king's offer of money or a better vineyard. His emphatic response to Ahab's request provides insight into Naboth's refusal. ***But Naboth said to Ahab, "The LORD forbid that I should give the inheritance of my fathers to you!"*** The Israelite principle, sent from God through Moses, of inalienable land ownership lay at the root of his vehement rejection of a seemingly attractive offer. This land allotted to individual tribes and families represented an immutable inheritance from God given according to His will. Therefore, only under the direst circumstances could land be leased for a certain period, but selling it or seizing it by force remained unlawful since the land ultimately belonged to God.[25]

Selling real estate would not constitute a good business pursuit in Israel since a family's inheritance and identity remained linked to their property. The senior members of any clan, both male and female, represented valuable repositories of information regarding "terrain, tools, climate, crop choices, livestock management, gardening, food processing, meal preparation, textile production," and more.[26] Carol Meyers states, "Family land was to be held in perpetuity. The identity of any family unit was thus inseparable from its land. The power of the agrarian mode to establish corporate identity as more important than individual freedom should not be underestimated. Perhaps none is so radical as the corporate identity and family solidarity of the early Israelite farm family as opposed to the achievement-oriented individualism of the industrialized West."[27]

Furthermore, a family's religion was at the core of their household culture and "a person's relationship to the deity was a function of that deity's connection to his or her family."[28] The king's attempted real estate transaction represented far more than a simple land transfer. Ahab essentially asked Naboth to sell his spiritual birthright and to abandon his family's identity passed from generation to generation. Naboth clearly understood the stakes involved, so he adamantly refused to sell his spiritual birthright or give up his family's identity and generational inheritance.

Ahab went home sullen and displeased because Naboth refused to follow Esau's example and sell out. The king threw one big pouting party. He got in bed, turned his face to the wall, and refused food. When Ahab did not appear for supper, Jezebel went to check on him. She asked, "What's the matter, and why are you too upset to eat?" Whining like a petulant child, the spoiled king told her of Naboth's refusal to sell his vineyard. Instantly, the evil queen reacted. Using an effective manipulation technique, she played upon his male ego and asked who was boss, "Are you not the king of Israel? Get up and eat something, and do not worry about a thing. I will get Naboth's vineyard for you" (my paraphrase). Walter Brueggemann notes that Jezebel's rhetorical question to Ahab represents "both a reprimand and an invitation," a reprimand for not behaving like a king and an invitation to exercise his royal power to seize the vineyard.[29]

As Jezebel's passive puppet, Ahab allowed his wicked wife to influence and guide his decisions. The queen gave commands, and the king obeyed. Burying his head in the pillow, Ahab willingly let her take control of the situation. Following in the legendary footsteps of her patron goddess, Anath, Jezebel did everything in her power to acquire the coveted vineyard. Usurping the king's authority, she wrote letters in Ahab's name, sealed them with the kingly seal, and then sent the missives to all the elders and nobles in Jezreel. This narrative truly showcases three types of dangerous characters: Ahab, a wicked, weak king; Jezebel, a wicked, strong queen; Jezreel's elders, wicked, subservient leaders. Aware of Jezebel's malevolent, murderous tactics, the men of the city followed her evil instructions without hesitation. Like Anath's father, El, in the mythology, not one man among them dared withstand this ferocious woman.

Her plot was treacherous down to each dastardly detail:

◆ Proclaim a fast to invoke impending calamity coming upon Israel and create the platform to present the innocent, unsuspecting scapegoat.

◆ Set Naboth in a visible place of honor among the people and then publicly destroy him.

◆ Seat two scoundrels across the table from Naboth who falsely accuse him of blaspheming God and the king.

◆ Then, take him out and stone him to death.

Rabbi Joseph Telushkin comments, "The conscienceless Jezebel devises a plot that breaches three of the Ten Commandments."[30] Firstly, she broke the ninth commandment, the prohibition against false witness, by using scoundrels to accuse Naboth of blasphemy falsely. Next, their lying set the stage to violate the sixth commandment, the prohibition against murder. Naboth's immediate conviction of blasphemy and treason resulted in his being stoned to death though he never committed the crime. Telushkin says, "Because people convicted of blasphemy and treason lose their estates as well as their lives, the queen rushes to her husband with the good news" of Naboth's death.[31] Ahab gleefully violated the eighth commandment, "which prohibits stealing," and took possession "of the coveted vineyard (his violation of the Tenth Commandment, which prohibits coveting one's neighbor's possessions, is what precipitated Jezebel's and Ahab's violation of the other three)."[32]

Hoffeditz and Yates also see that the particularly heinous nature of Jezebel's crime involved her strategy to use "the Torah to break the Torah. To counter Naboth's Torah-based claim" that forbade the selling of property associated with the family inheritance, Jezebel instigated a legal charge of Torah violation by accusing Naboth of blasphemy against God and the king.[33] She satisfied the Torah requirement of "two witnesses for a capital crime" and then violated the Torah "by suborning perjury and presenting false testimony."[34]

After receiving word of Naboth's death, Jezebel sashayed into the king's room and told him to get up and take possession of the coveted vineyard. Ahab went at once to claim his ill-gotten prize, but God had seen every occurrence that fateful day in Jezreel. Such wickedness would not go unpunished. Additionally, II Kings 9:25-26 indicates their crime far exceeded the senseless murder of one innocent man, ***Then Jehu said to Bidkar his captain, "Pick him up, and throw him into the tract of the field of Naboth the Jezreelite; for remember, when you and I were riding together behind Ahab his father, that the***

LORD *laid this burden upon him: 'Surely I saw yesterday the blood of Naboth* <u>and the blood of his sons,</u>*' says the LORD, 'and I will repay you in this plot,' says the LORD. Now therefore, take and throw him on the plot of ground, according to the word of the LORD"* (my emphasis). It appears they also murdered Naboth's entire family to ensure there were no remaining heirs to lay claim to the family property.

God sent Elijah to meet the king and give him a divine announcement of doom, *"This is what the LORD says: Wasn't it enough that you killed Naboth? Must you rob him too? Because you have done this, dogs will lick your blood at the very place where they licked the blood of Naboth!"*[35] When Ahab looked up and saw Elijah's familiar face, the joy over his new possession evaporated into thin air, and he exclaimed, *"So, my enemy, you found me!" "Yes,"* Elijah responded, *"I have come because you have sold yourself to do what is evil in the LORD'S sight."*

Fearlessly, the old prophet pronounced judgement on Ahab and his entire house, *"So now the Lord says, 'I will bring disaster on you and consume you. I will destroy every one of your male descendants, slave and free alike, anywhere in Israel! I am going to destroy your family as I did the family of Jeroboam son of Nebat and the family of Baasha son of Ahijah, for you have made me very angry and have led Israel into sin.' And regarding Jezebel, the Lord says, 'Dogs will eat Jezebel's body at the plot of land in Jezreel. The members of Ahab's family who die in the city will be eaten by dogs, and those who die in the field will be eaten by vultures.'"*[36] Rabbi Telushkin states, "Elijah's three-word condemnation of Ahab, *Ha-ratzakhta ve-gam yarashta?*—'Have you murdered and also inherited?' —remains perhaps the most powerful denunciation of an evil person in the entire Hebrew Bible."[37]

Upon hearing the impending judgment for his sin, Ahab repented by humbling himself with fasting and mourning before the Lord. Despite rending his garments and fasting, Ahab's repentance seemed somewhat shallow and insincere since he still retained possession of the stolen vineyard.[38] Second Kings 9:21 indicates the field passed to Ahab's son, King Jehoram. Telushkin says, "Still, Ahab's act of abasement prompts God to postpone the eradication of his house to the time of his equally evil son."[39]

Nevertheless, Jezebel remained unfazed by the prophet's pronouncement and continued her idolatrous ways to the end. Many years after Ahab's death, Jehu, anointed by Elisha's aide, staged a coup against Jehoram, Ahab's son. After slaying King Jehoram and Ahaziah, king of Judah, Jehu confronted Jezebel, who attempted to seduce him. Painting herself like a prostitute of Baal and putting on her royal tiara, she gazed wantonly out the window but to no avail. Then, Jezebel desperately tried to intimidate and manipulate Jehu with a bit of psychology. *"Have you come in peace, you murderer? You're just like Zimri, who murdered his master!"* (NLT) Talk about the pot calling the kettle black! Jezebel was the murderess-in-chief.

Undeterred, Jehu refused to be intimidated or manipulated by this brazen woman, and he asked who was on his side. When two or three eunuchs showed their support, he directed them to hurl her from the palace window. Badly injured by the fall, Jezebel was trampled by Jehu's horses and died. The evil queen assassinated many others, including Naboth and God's prophets; now, she suffered the same fate. The new king sat to a feast; then after eating and drinking, he instructed his servants to find Jezebel and bury her, *"Someone go bury this cursed woman, for she is the daughter of a king."*[40]

The soldiers went outside to look for her, but they found only Jezebel's skull, hands, and feet because ravenous dogs had consumed the rest. Evidently, many people knew about Elijah's curse against Jezebel because when the men reported to Jehu, he stated, *"This fulfills the message from the LORD, which he spoke through his servant Elijah from Tishbe, 'At the plot of land in Jezreel, dogs will eat Jezebel's body. Her remains will be scattered like dung on the plot of land in Jezreel, so that no one will be able to recognize her.' "*[41] Groningen notes that no tombstone was set up to mark her resting place or to keep her name in remembrance; thus, confirming the Lord's word.[42] In that ancient Middle Eastern culture, remaining unburied represented a terrible fate.[43]

Regrettably, the intimidating, manipulating, assassinating spirit of Jezebel lived on in her daughter, Athaliah. Indeed, this evil spirit compounded in the next generation and produced a beastly woman who killed her own grandchildren in a brutal power grab to seize the throne of Judah. Groningen chronicles, "Athaliah, mother of Ahaziah and daughter of Ahab and Jezebel, angered by the death of her son, attempts to destroy the entire Davidic house."[44] As queen mother, she retained power and influence and used it to remove any opposition to her efforts to rule Judah. Just "as Jehu destroyed Baalism and its royal supporters in Israel, so Athaliah attempts to destroy the worship of the Lord."[45] Furthermore, the actions of Athaliah reveal the enemy's ultimate goal of wiping out the messianic line to stop the prophetic fulfillment of the promised Redeemer.

Thankfully, her satanically inspired efforts failed when a righteous woman refused to stand by and let Athaliah annihilate the royal seed with its messianic promise. Second Kings 11:2 says, **But Ahaziah's sister Jehosheba, the daughter of King Jehoram, took Ahaziah's infant son, Joash, and stole him away from among the rest of the king's children, who were about to be killed. She put Joash and his nurse in a bedroom, and they hid him from Athaliah, so the child was not murdered** (NLT). Jehosheba, daughter of King Jehoram and sister of Ahaziah, was possibly Athaliah's daughter, but she refused to follow her mother's evil footsteps. This courageous king's daughter was not intimidated or manipulated, and she did not allow Joash to be assassinated. Jehosheba stepped up, risked her life, rescued the covenant child, and stopped the enemy's deadly plan in its tracks. God's redemptive promise remained alive and well. On the other hand, Athaliah suffered a fate similar to her mother because in the end, the spirit of Jezebel brings destruction to those governed by it. Be a king's daughter like Jehosheba, not like Jezebel!

Chapter Three Footnotes:

1. Lawrence O. Richards, *Complete Bible Handbook* (Waco, TX: Word Books, 1987), 197.

2. Janet Howe Gaines, "How Bad Was Jezebel?" biblicalarchaeology.org, 3/22/22, https://www.biblicalarchaeology.org/daily/people-cultures-in-the-bible/people-in-the-bible/how-bad-was-jezebel/

3. Ibid.

4. Ibid.

5. Ibid.

6. Ibid.

7. Thomas Cahill, *The Gifts of the Jews: How a Tribe of Desert Nomads Changed the Way Everyone Thinks and Feels* (New York, NY: Anchor Books, 1998), 173.

8. Ibid.

9. A. Brenner, *The Israelite Woman: Social Role and Literary Type in Biblical Narrative* (Biblical Seminar 2; Sheffield: JSOT Press, 1994), 26.

10. David M. Hoffeditz and Gary E. Yates, "Femme Fatale *Redux: Intertextual Connection to Elijah/ Jezebel Narratives in Mark 6:14-29," Bulletin for Biblical Research* 15/2 2005: 202.

11. Gerard Van Groningen, "1-2 Kings," in *Evangelical Commentary on the Bible*, ed. Walter A. Elwell, (Grand Rapids: Baker Books, 2001), 246.

12. Ibid.

13. Merrill F. Unger, *The New Unger's Bible Handbook*, Revised by Gary N. Larson (Chicago, IL: Moody Press, 1984), 169.

14. Ibid.

15. J. I. Packer and M. C. Tenney, eds., *Illustrated Manners and Customs of the Bible* (Nashville, TN: Thomas Nelson Publishers, 1980), 144.

16. Ibid.

17. Ibid.

18. I Kings 17:10-14, *The Message*.

19. Groningen, *Evangelical Commentary*, 247.

20. Ibid.

21. Hoffeditz and Yates, Femme Fatale, 203.

22. Craig S. Keener, *The IVP Bible Background Commentary: New Testament* (Downers Grove,

IL: InterVarsity Press, 1993), 703.

23. Hoffeditz and Yates, Femme Fatale, 202.

24. Packer and Tenney, *Illustrated Manners and Customs*, 144.

25. Ibid.

26. See Leviticus 25:23, 25; Numbers 36:7; Ezekiel 46:18.

27. Leo G. Perdue, et al., *Families in Ancient Israel* (Louisville, KY: Westminster John Knox Press, 1997), 30.

28. Ibid., 19, 21-22.

29. Ibid., 39.

30. Walter Brueggemann, *1 and 2 Kings* (Smith and Helwys Bible Commentary; Macon, GA: Smith & Helwys, 2000), 259.

31. Rabbi Joseph Telushkin, *Biblical Literacy: The Most Important People, Events, and Ideas of the Hebrew Bible* (New York, NY: HarperCollins, 1997), 259.

32. Ibid.

33. Ibid.

34. Hoffeditz and Yates, Femme Fatale, 206.

35. Ibid.

36. I Kings 21:19, NLT.

37. I Kings 21:21-24, NLT.

38. Telushkin, *Biblical Literacy*, 260.

39. Ibid.

40. Ibid.

41. II Kings 9:34, NLT.

42. II Kings 9:36-37, NLT.

43. Groningen, *Evangelical Commentary*, 255.

44. Perdue, et al., *Families*, 176.

45. Groningen, *Evangelical Commentary*, 255.

46. Ibid.

Priceless and Protected

Meekness is not weakness. It is power under control.
— Warren W. Wiersbe

According to Bill Farmer's newspaper column, J. Upton Dickson, a fun-loving fellow, talked about writing a book entitled *Cower Power*. He also founded a group of submissive people called DOORMATS. That stands for 'Dependent Organization of Really Meek and Timid Souls'—if there are no objections. Their motto was "the meek shall inherit the earth"— if that is okay with everybody. The symbol for the DOORMAT group was the yellow traffic light.[1]

Mr. Dickson's concept of meekness represents a common perception: someone who is timid, spineless, unassertive, easily dominated, or intimidated; a veritable Casper Milquetoast who speaks softly and gets hit with a big stick. Many, even in the church, believe meekness equates to weakness. Synonyms for meekness include timidity, fearfulness, compliance, weakness, tameness, and docility. None of these words sound like attractive traits worth pursuing. Yet in Matthew 5:5, Jesus pronounced a blessing upon individuals who exhibit this attribute: ***Blessed are the meek, For they shall inherit the earth.*** This verse alludes to a promise made in Psalm 37:11, ***But the meek shall inherit the earth, And shall delight themselves in the abundance of peace.***

Jesus used this word as a descriptor of Himself as well in Matthew 11:29 (KJV). Peter admonished us to follow Jesus' example and wrote in I Peter 2:23, *Who, when He was reviled, did not revile in return; when He suffered, He did not threaten, but committed Himself to Him who judges righteously*. Jesus demonstrated self-effacement of His own interests and willingly laid down His life for us.[2] He said in John 10:17-18, *Therefore My Father loves Me, because I lay down My life that I may take it again. No one takes it from Me, but I lay it down of Myself. I have power to lay it down, and I have power to take it again. This command I have received from My Father*. On the cross, He prayed for forgiveness for those who crucified Him. Conversely, He remained "defiant towards the religious establishment in defending the helpless and diseased as well as opposing evil."[3] In Matthew 26:53-54, Jesus stated His ability to call for twelve legions of angels to save Him from the cross, but His exercise of that power would have thwarted the fulfillment of Scripture. Was His meekness indicative of weakness or controlled power?

Moses provides another biblical example of meekness. Numbers 12:3 (KJV) says he was very meek, more than all men upon the earth. The life of Moses provides clear evidence that meekness is not weakness but strength under control. He stood up to Pharaoh and exercised fearless leadership against continual stubbornness amongst his followers. Moses defended his right to lead when his authority was challenged. He held his place as "the most visible and powerful figure in the traveling nation of Israel."[4] Moses never operated under the presumption of self-reliance, nor did he ever leverage his position for self-aggrandizement. Instead, he relied on God's strength and often fell on his face before the Lord when others withstood him.[5] Moses' disobedience in striking the rock instead of speaking to it and then self-importantly proclaiming his ability to bring forth water represents the major exception. His behavior on this occasion remains incongruous with the tenor of his life and serves "as a foil to highlight the prevailing quality of meekness in Moses' demeanor."[6]

So what exactly is meekness, this quality that Jesus said bestows an amazing inheritance? "The key to understanding the virtue of meekness is that it is not a quality of weakness but rather of strength. Meekness is not cowardice, timidity, or lack of confidence."[7] Meekness is derived from the classical Greek word "used to describe tame animals, soothing medicine, and a gentle breeze. The word also implies self-control."[8] This biblical ideal stands in contrast to humanistic philosophies influenced by Greco-Roman classicism. Much of the world's literature exalts the conquering hero or heroine "who refuses to submit and who exerts his or her interests against anyone who might challenge those interests. Most cultures reserve their rewards for the people who compete successfully through strength of will and superior power."[9] Within this context, Jesus' portrait of an ideal disciple modeling meekness represents a stark contradiction to conventional wisdom.[10]

The adage "strong enough to be gentle" comes close to defining this Christlike quality. Geoffrey B. Wilson remarked, "Meekness is the mark of a man [or woman] who has been mastered by God." Meekness and gentleness remain "robustly positive virtues, not a display of passive timidity."[11] Contrasting these qualities with opposite behaviors provides an even clearer understanding of their nature. "Meekness and gentleness are the opposite of harshness, a grasping spirit, vengefulness, self-aggrandizement, and lack of self-control."[12]

First Peter 3:4 admonishes godly women to clothe themselves with this beautiful inner quality, the unfading beauty of a meek and quiet spirit, which is priceless in God's sight. Obviously, a meek and quiet spirit exemplifies the exact opposite of the spirit of Jezebel outlined in the previous chapter. The spirit of Jezebel runs roughshod over anything or anyone standing in the way of getting its way. This calculating spirit intimidates, manipulates, and assassinates. Just like the thief referenced in

John 10:10, the Jezebel spirit steals, kills, and destroys. It rejects God, exalts idolatry, destroys nations, murders God's people, silences the prophets, normalizes perversion, and wipes out entire families, including its own. Jezebel the prophetess referenced in Revelation 2:20-23 presents a modern manifestation of the ancient influence that rejects righteousness and leads God's people astray into worldliness. James 4:4 confronts this evil attempt to join the holy with the profane, *Adulterers and adulteresses! Do you not know that friendship with the world is enmity with God? Whoever therefore wants to be a friend of the world makes himself an enemy of God*.

The Jezebel spirit stands in stark contrast to the unfading beauty of the gentle, quiet spirit treasured by God. According to Rick Renner, *meek* comes from the Greek word *praus*, "a word that describes *the attitude of one who is friendly, warm, forbearing, patient, kind, and gentle.*"[13] Peter's use of the word, *praus*, pictures someone the exact opposite of an angry, temperamental, volatile person who flies off the handle. Proverbs 31:26 describes this kind of lady, *She opens her mouth with wisdom, And on her tongue is the law of kindness*. Even when faced with unfair treatment, a meek person chooses to respond correctly by exercising self-control, exhibiting gentleness, and extending forgiveness. T. F. Tenney said, "Meekness is to endure injury without resentment." This sort of response goes contrary to the flesh and requires extreme control over one's actions and reactions. Meekness equates to self-mastery.

Peter also used the word, *quiet*, to describe this valuable inner adornment. He employed the Greek *hēsychios*, which delineates a person with the ability to calm his/herself "*and to maintain a state of peace and tranquility*."[14] Instead of angrily exploding and saying things he/she will later regret, this individual remains quiet and refrains from responding in anger. Practicing quietness reflects a deliberate decision to make peace instead of contributing to conflict. Isaiah 30:15 says our strength is found in quietness and confidence. John Bunyan wisely observed, "If we have not quiet in our minds, outward comfort will do no more for us than a golden slipper on a gouty foot."

The wise man wrote in Proverbs 26:23, *Fervent lips with a wicked heart Are like earthenware covered with silver dross*. *Fervent* comes from the Hebrew word, *dālaq*, meaning "to kindle or inflame," referring to words that kindle strife and stir up situations. This verse mirrors James 3:5, *Even so the tongue is a little member and boasts great things. See how great a forest a little fire kindles!* When Peter wrote about having a meek and quiet spirit, he described a woman "so strong in spirit" she could refrain from these angry outbursts and be "a calming force in a variety of difficult situations."[15] She "steadies the ship" and keeps the peace. It requires great strength to retain the quality of quietness. It is much easier to pop off and give someone a piece of your mind. It may be satisfying in the moment, but the urge to give someone a piece of your mind might cost you peace of mind. Renner rightly observes, "A woman who continually controls herself"—holds her temper, keeps a lid on her emotions, and remains a stable, tranquil force in every situation—demonstrates "evidence of great maturity."[16] God views this kind of woman as rare, precious, dear, and valuable.[17]

This attractiveness comes from the inside out and transcends any earthly beauty treatment and physical adornment. Craig Keener states, "Ancients considered a meek and quiet spirit a prime virtue for women, and many moralists advised this attitude instead of dressing in the latest fashions to attract men's attention, a vice commonly attributed to aristocratic women but imitated by those who could afford to do so."[18] This fashion statement never goes out of style! Peter described this exquisite quality as incorruptible or unfading, meaning this kind of beauty does not fade as we grow older and our bodies age. Botox and cosmetic surgery cannot confer this level of loveliness or maintain its effects.

Truly, the most priceless ornament in the universe is not the renowned Hope diamond or the Cullinan I, a magnificent

530.2-carat, pear-shaped diamond in the possession of the queen of England. One day, those diamonds will dissolve, but an attractive inner attitude lasts eternally. First Peter 3:5 says holy women of old adorned themselves in this manner by trusting God and accepting the authority of their husbands. The ability to adorn yourself in this manner comes from trusting in God instead of expecting your husband to be your ultimate source of fulfillment. Too often, women depend on their spouses to fulfill all their emotional needs, but this expectation is too great for any human to accomplish. Psalm 16:11 explains that fullness of joy comes from God's presence, and pleasures await at His right hand, the exclusive place of favor.

Peter invoked Sarah as an example of a woman who trusted God and honored her husband even though his actions were sometimes less than honorable towards her. It seems the apostle provided a clue to her ability to remain very beautiful long after others were past their flower. Granted, this Scripture passage runs directly contrary to modern-day feminism and its quest for female dominance as covered in previous chapters. Keener comments, "In contrast to many of the current models in Roman high society," Peter appealed to Sarah, a prominent matriarch, extolled for her "piety in Jewish tradition."[19] Sarah's story yields some valuable lessons regarding God's response to women who place their trust in Him even when faced with unfair treatment and subjected to dangerous circumstances. Perhaps women might quip to their husbands, "When you act like Abraham, I'll act like Sarah." Abraham, however, did not exemplify a model husband despite his calling as the father of the faithful. At times, he was self-seeking and lacking in care towards his wife as we shall see.

Sarah's first appearance in Scripture comes near the end of a long genealogy in Genesis 11:10-32. We tend to skip these 'boring' passages, but they often provide important clues. The segment containing Sarah's name "drops early clues" that her identity was lost in a world of men.[20] Genesis 11:27 introduces

Terah and his family; thus, narrowing the focus of biblical history to this family from Ur of the Chaldees in Mesopotamia, located in modern-day southern Iraq. The narrative focuses on Sarah's father and three brothers, Abraham, Nahor, and Haran, and their descendants. Yet Sarah's true place in the family remains obscured until twenty-four years later "when Abraham got into a predicament and told everyone she was his half-sister" from a different mother.[21] Carolyn Custis James notes that the genealogy dropped Sarah "from her high-ranking position as Terah's daughter" when the family registry identified her "as *Abraham's wife*," implying a familial connection "solely by marriage."[22] Entering Sarah into the genealogy in this manner reflects a patriarchal culture that viewed daughters as less valuable than sons and tied a woman's identity to her husband.[23]

Then, seemingly adding insult to injury, verse thirty highlights Sarah's barrenness, ***But Sarai was barren; she had no child***. Instead of according her honor, the first descriptor emphasized Sarah's shame due to her inability to produce children. In the ancient Near East, the number of a woman's sons constituted her value; therefore, "Sarah scored a zero."[24] As a barren woman lost in a man's world, Sarah had two strikes against her, seemingly with no role in God's redemptive purposes. For twenty-four long years, she waited in vain for a child. During this time, Abraham moved his family into a danger zone, where he feared for his life because of his wife's beauty. Without regard for Sarah's safety, Abraham instructed her to tell a half-truth and say he was her brother to save his skin. Genesis 12:13 illustrates his extreme selfishness, ***"Then they will spare my life and treat me well because of their interest in you"*** (NLT). What about Sarah's life? What kind of treatment would she receive from the men interested in her? It appears Abraham did not care what happened to her as long as he remained safe. Sarah was just a pawn in a man's world.

Sarah complied with Abraham's selfish instructions and put her neck on the block twice to save his.[25] First, Pharaoh took

Sarah, and King Abimelech of Gerar took her years later. What kind of husband would subject his wife to that? Abraham may not have valued Sarah as he should, but she remained valuable to God. When Abraham placed her life in danger, the Lord did not abandon Sarah. Remember, a meek and quiet spirit remains *priceless* in His sight, and God always *protects* what is precious to Him. Carolyn Custis James states, "Amazingly, Sarah was the *first* person to taste the blessings of God's covenant. Pharaoh learned to his dismay that Sarah was the apple of God's eye when He lashed out against the Egyptian ruler's household with a terrible plague 'because of Sarai, Abram's wife' (Genesis 12:17). Later, God's threatening words to Abimelech, 'You're as good as dead' (Genesis 20:3) sent this chilling, unambiguous message: Lay a hand on Sarah and you will reckon with God."[26] Just think, against this patriarchal backdrop that devalued women and viewed them as expendable property, God demonstrated how much He honored and valued her. God delivered Sarah for her sake, not for Abraham's, because she had a vital role to play in His redemptive purposes.

On God's wall of family portraits, Sarah's picture hung alongside her father and brothers. Her frame did not remain empty until she had a child. On the contrary, Sarah was a true part of God's family, a daughter, not an in-law, "born to bear God's image, born to advance His cause."[27] As God's image bearer, her identity remained anchored in Him "and nothing could ever take that away from her."[28] The Lord's love encircled Sarah even in her most vulnerable moments—in His sight, she was both *priceless and protected!*

In time, Sarah's day for promise fulfillment finally arrived when the Lord appeared at their family compound along with two other men. While Abraham showed hospitality to the three mysterious strangers, Sarah remained secluded in her tent, out of sight "but stealthily within earshot of the men's conversation—which makes me love her all the more."[29] The One who knows all knew she eavesdropped, and He had a word for Sarah.

As the conversation progressed, He directly addressed her deepest desire, one she abandoned long ago, *"I will certainly return to you according to the time of life, and behold, Sarah your wife shall have a son."*[30]

As various emotions poured over Sarah, she laughed, but the One who called her by name knew all about her. Yahweh knew her incredulity as well as her despair, her shame, her sorrow, and unbelief.[31] He knew the sound of her incredulous inner laughter even though she fearfully denied it. Sarah, so defeated by her circumstances, had forgotten God's power to save and deliver but "He brought her to the end of her hopes to bring her to himself."[32] He asked, *"Is anything too hard for the LORD?"* The Lord kept His word and did for Sarah exactly as He promised, *For Sarah conceived and bore Abraham a son in his old age, at the set time of which God had spoken to him.*[33]

Holding her promised child, ninety-year-old Sarah proclaimed in Genesis 21:6, *"God has made me laugh, and all who hear will laugh with me."* Her laughter was a long time coming, but now "she had solid physical evidence that *nothing* was too hard for the Lord," a beautiful and fitting climax to an interminable weary road.[34] Indeed, Sarah's story speaks to us all. Carolyn Custis James states, "Despite her failings (which ought to endear her to us more than if she were some paragon of perfection), Sarah left behind a strong legacy of faith and a powerful message for the church."[35] Hebrews 11:11 places Sarah's portrait of honor in Faith's Hall of Fame; thus, erasing her shame, *By faith Sarah herself also received strength to conceive seed, and she bore a child when she was past the age, because she judged Him faithful who had promised.* Her story provides reassurance "that we have a vital place in God's purposes, that he values us and is at work in our lives."[36] First Peter 3:6 reminds us we are Sarah's daughters if we do what is right even when things are not right, not fearing any terrifying situation. Just as God faithfully took care of Sarah, we can trust Him to care for us because we are also *priceless and protected.*

<u>Chapter Four Footnotes:</u>

1. Illustrations on Meekness, bible.org
https://bible.org/node/11449

2. Leland Ryken, James C. Wilhoit, and Tremper Longman III, eds., *Dictionary of Biblical Imagery: An Encyclopedic Exploration of the Images, Symbols, Motifs, Metaphors, Figures of Speech and Literary Patterns of the Bible* (Downers Grove, IL: IVP Academic, 1998), 546.

3. Ibid.

4. Ibid.

5. Numbers 14:5; 16:4, 22, 45; 20:6.

6. Ryken, Wilhoit, and Longman, eds., *Dictionary of Biblical Imagery*, 546.

7. Ibid., 545.

8. Ibid.

9. Ibid.

10. Ibid.

11. Ibid., 546.

12. Ibid.

13. Rick Renner, *Sparkling Gems from the Greek: 365 Greek Word Studies for Every Day of the Year To Sharpen Your Understanding of God's Word*

(Tulsa, OK: Teach All Nations Printing, 2003), 754, italics original.

14. Ibid., italics original.

15. Ibid.

16. Ibid.

17. Ibid.

18. Keener, *The IVP Bible Background Commentary*, 716.

19. Ibid.

20. Carolyn Custis James, *Lost Women of the Bible: The Women We Thought We Knew* (Grand Rapids, MI: Zondervan, 2005), 67.

21. Ibid.

22. Ibid., italics original.

23. Ibid.

24. Ibid., 68.

25. Ibid., 69.

26. Ibid., 79, italics original.

27. Ibid.

28. Ibid.

29. Ibid., 76.

30. Genesis 18:10.

31. James, *Lost Women*, 77.

32. Ibid.

33. Genesis 21:2.

34. James, *Lost Women*, 77, italics original.

35. Ibid.

36. Ibid., 82.

The True Face of Submission

In submission we are free to value other people. Their dreams and plans become important to us. We have entered into a new, wonderful, glorious freedom, the freedom to give up our own rights for the good of others.

—Richard J. Foster

Richard Foster's statement connects submission with freedom, but most probably consider submission and freedom as polar opposites. People often associate submission with subjugation and bondage rather than liberty. A common concept regarding submission entails compliant people exuding 'cower power' and belonging to J. Upton Dickson's DOORMATS club referenced in the previous chapter. Consequently, submission gets a bad rap similar to the widespread misperceptions about meekness previously discussed.

It seems most people see submission through the lens of the curse spoken in Genesis 3:16, *"I will greatly multiply your sorrow and your conception; In pain you shall bring forth children; Your desire shall be for your husband, And he shall rule over you."* David Norris, however, rightly observes this relational dysfunction was descriptive of what would be rather than prescriptive of what should be.[1] Instead of reacting joyfully to the woman's yearning for emotional intimacy, the man defaulted to a domineering style of leadership.[2] "For Eve, it embodied the same death principle that enslaved Adam to the soil. Male domination and female subordination do not exemplify God's ideal."[3] Contrariwise, these default human responses represent perpetual relational fallout in a broken world in need of redemption.

Unfortunately, it appears many have gleaned the wrong pieces of the story in Eden's hasty evacuation.[4] The curse rather than the Creation often drives the theological narrative of the male/female relational model. If Jesus came to redeem us from the curse, why would we operate from this faulty premise? Nevertheless, when the curse influences the church's view of submission, many Christians embrace selective patriarchy, and this creates a constant struggle to preserve certain aspects of a relational system rooted in humanity's fallenness.[5] Their sincere but misguided preservation attempts can result in ill-advised actions that run counter to biblical submission.

As a lady minister, I experienced this reality on more than one occasion, especially when stepping into the pulpit to preach. People who espouse a patriarchal version of submission rooted in the Genesis curse make a show of walking out and refusing to listen to my message, citing my lack of submission to explain their actions. In truth, however, when a pastor invites me to minister in his church, I am operating in submission to his authority while those who walk out manifest opposition to pastoral authority. It is interesting to note that other women often exhibit the fiercest resistance in this regard. Ironically, under the banner of their supposed 'submission,' these women drag their husbands and families out of the church service with them. Thus, their understanding of submission, convoluted by the curse, causes them to view submission as rebellion and rebellion as submission.

Others adopt the "tiebreaker approach" to submission like the man who said he and his wife usually agree, but on the rare occasions they do not, he asks her to submit.[6] He views submission as a biblical tiebreaking tool to resolve marital deadlock. Carolyn Custis James says, "Like the fire extinguisher collecting dust in the closet, his version of submission remains conveniently within reach in case of emergency and quickly puts out sparks that if left unchecked might burst into flame."[7] At times, however, invoking the so-called tiebreaker rule can leave women smoldering with resentment. They are like "the young wife (who evidently hadn't yet mastered the art of giving in)," and when asked how married life suited her, she "admitted feeling 'oppressed, repressed, suppressed, and depressed.' "[8] Is her negative response indicative of God's idea of submission and plan for marriage? Why would any woman want to marry if that sort of submission is the price of admission?[9]

In the fog of confusion, it can be "tempting to side with those who are convinced that submission is an outdated convention—okay for previous generations perhaps, but passé in today's world."[10] They view submission as an old-fashioned, outdated concept practiced by people who are out of touch with female advancement and unwilling to move forward into a changing world. Regardless of our views, the New Testament issues a call to submission written on its pages in black and white. James notes, "Advocates on both sides of the discussion express concern" about potential abuses but the fact remains "that the Bible clearly teaches submission."[11] Given the brutal reality of human brokenness, relational fallout, and resultant abuse, should we adopt "a kinder, gentler version of submission? Or does the Bible's version of submission (which surprisingly addresses both men and women) take us to a whole new realm of human relationships?"[12] Perhaps our defective definitions trivialize biblical submission and obscure its *true face*. Maybe we need to look anew at this vital theological theme to gain greater insight and deeper understanding.

Let us begin by considering the meaning of mutual submission that grounds the biblical teaching on this subject. Stephen Beck offers the following personal experience to illustrate this key concept:

Driving down a country road, I came to a very narrow bridge. In front of the bridge, a sign was posted: "YIELD." Seeing no oncoming cars, I continued across the bridge and headed to my destination. On the way back, I came to the same one-lane bridge, approaching it from the other direction. To my surprise, I saw another YIELD sign posted. Curious, I thought, "I'm sure there was one posted on the other side." Upon reaching the other side of the bridge I looked back. Sure enough, yield signs were placed at each end of the bridge. Drivers from both directions were requested to give right of way as a reasonable and gracious way of preventing a head-on collision. When the Bible instructs Christians to "be subject to one another" (Ephesians 5:21) it is simply a reasonable and gracious command to let the other have the right of way and avoid interpersonal head-on collisions.[13]

What a great analogy! Peter offered a similar admonition in I Peter 5:5, *Likewise you younger people, submit yourselves to your elders. Yes, all of you be submissive to one another, and be clothed with humility, for "God resists the proud, But gives grace to the humble."* The apostle's "instruction would have seemed positively countercultural to Peter's readers, as humility was so often seen in Greco-Roman culture as a mark of a slave."[14] Paul called us to walk the same path of submissive humility in Philippians 2:3-4, *Let nothing be done through selfish ambition or conceit, but in lowliness of mind let each esteem others better than himself. Let each of you look out not only for his own interests, but also for the interests of others.*

True humility, as opposed to a contrived, self-degrading humiliation, flows from recognizing

> *one's complete dependence on God and is ex-*
> *pressed by the acceptance of one's role and*
> *position in God's economy. With such humility*
> *one is freed from attempts to gain more power*
> *or prestige. Instead, humility expresses itself in*
> *the willingness to serve others even beyond*
> *one's self-interest* (Jobes 2005: 309).[15]

Humility displays a key part of biblical submission. Humility is not thinking less of yourself; it is thinking of yourself less. Maggie Ross nicely sums it up, "The Body of Christ is the fundamental resonance of humility, of self-giving, that is sacrificial *kenosis* [self-emptying] that leads to creation and re-creation, no matter in what sphere. It is the cohesion of creation."

Ephesians 5:21 highlights another essential component of mutual submission, ***Submitting to one another in the fear of God*** (my emphasis). Paul enjoined that submission be carried out in the fear of God. Craig Keener observes, "Someone who keeps in mind that he or she has a Lord in heaven is not likely to lord it over others, but to take more willingly his or her place as a servant—whether the world views them as master or servant."[16] Fear of God, humility, yielding, esteeming others, and putting them first—all these qualities undergird the New Testament call to mutual submission and provide proper understanding of Ephesians 5:21-33. This passage does not promote male domination and female subjugation. On the contrary, Paul called for mutual submission in the fear of God coupled with love, humility, unselfishness, and respect.

Reading Scripture through a Western lens and interpreting it against the backdrop of our current culture skew our ability to grasp Paul's countercultural admonition in these household codes. In Greco-Roman culture, a man's wife, children, and slaves were considered his property, and his authority included the power of life and death. When a child was born, a father could choose to keep the baby or, if he did not want the infant, to condemn it to death by exposure to the elements. Christopher Perry writes, "Roman culture was androcentric and as such, male superiority and domination defined all familial relationships."[17] Thus, Keener points out the radical nature of Paul's call for mutual submission in Ephesians 5:21, "Although it was customary to call on wives, children, and slaves to submit in various ways, to call *all* members of a group (including the *paterfamilias*, the male head of the household) to submit to one another was unheard-of."[18]

Paul's admonition for wifely submission must be studied within the context of mutual submission because it underscores the fact that his definition differed from the surrounding culture. Her submission is **as to the Lord**; thus, the wife's love for the Lord influences her relationship with her husband. The Amplified Bible offers this excellent insight, "She submits to her husband, not to men in general; not as inferior to him, nor in violation of her Christian ethics, but honoring her husband as protector and head of the home, respecting the responsibility of his position and his accountability to God." A skilled teacher, Paul cited "the most authoritative role models available to him: Christ as lover and the church as submitter" to demonstrate the proper dynamics of the marriage relationship.[19] Paul grounded his definition of submission "in terms of mutual service" by calling "on husbands to love their wives in such a radical way that husbands become their wives' servants too."[20] Therefore, the outcome of submission results in service to others instead of power exercised over them.

The English language has only one word for *love* while the Greek language uses several different terms. *Eros* refers to romantic or sexual love; *storgē* speaks of familial love such as parental love for a child; *phileō* describes brotherly love or friendship; and *agapē* defines the highest form of sacrificial love for the one loved. Paul enjoined husbands to love their wives with *agape* love, the highest form of sacrificial love. Perry further notes the countercultural nature of Ephesians 5:25,

"It is striking and even shocking that Paul has instructed husbands to ἀγαπάω (love) their wives."[21] His contemporaries "expected him to say husbands should rule or govern their wives."[22] Instead, Paul instructed them to afford their wives the same treatment extended to their honorable male peers. According to the New Testament scholar, Clinton Arnold, men were "never instructed to love their wives" except in these New Testament household codes.[23]

In contrast to most ancient writers, Paul's household codes in Ephesians 5 devote more space exhorting husbands to love their wives than focusing on wives' submission. His exhortation for wifely submission "stands out more strongly" in our Western culture, but his admonition for husbands to love their wives rather than rule them "would have stood out more strongly" in his culture.[24] Keener points out that Paul never addressed "the husband's role in the wife's submission; he does not urge the husband to inculcate submission" in her.[25] Paul simply instructed the husband to serve his wife in the same manner as "Christ served the church" and to love her as his own body.[26] Keener further notes that Paul explicitly defined Christ's love "in terms of self-sacrificial service, not in terms of his authority (5:23-27). Of course, authoritarian leadership on *any* basis conflicts with the teaching and example of Jesus throughout the Gospels, so those who advocate it today would do well to consider whether they grieve the Spirit of God."[27]

Moreover, the imagery of head and body stresses "that husband and wife should see themselves as one and work together with a common purpose and goal."[28] In contrast to most codes addressed "only to the male householder," Paul addressed each member, instructing both husbands and wives to do their part and not "use his letter to enforce the other person's part."[29] Finally, verse 33 sums up his definition of mutual submission within marriage, ***However, each man among you*** [without exception] ***is to love his wife as his very own self*** [with behavior worthy of respect and esteem, always seeking the best for her with an attitude of lovingkindness], *and the wife* [must see to it] *that she respects and delights in her husband* [that she notices him and prefers him and treats him with loving concern, treasuring him, honoring him, and holding him dear]" (Amplified Bible). Paul's summary of mutual submission contains nary a whiff of male domination or female subjugation. Indeed, using "the most socially acceptable language of his day," Paul made his case "that both partners must seek to serve one another because of Christ's reign in their lives."[30]

The story of Mary and Joseph, usually relegated to annual Christmas programs and pageants, offers perhaps one of the greatest biblical examples of this sort of mutual love and respect *as unto the Lord*. Luke 1:26-28 recounts, *Now in the sixth month the angel Gabriel was sent by God to a city of Galilee named Nazareth, to a virgin betrothed to a man whose name was Joseph, of the house of David. The virgin's name was Mary. And having come in, the angel said to her, "Rejoice, highly favored one, the Lord is with you; blessed are you among women!"* Carolyn Custis James notes, "With those words, Mary lost her reputation, her dreams, and the respect of the Jewish community. At least initially, she lost the trust of her husband-to-be."[31] Furthermore, what did her parents think of her outlandish claim of miraculous immaculate conception? The angel's words radically altered the course of Mary's life and shattered any girlish hopes or dreams of a normal married life with Joseph.[32]

At first, Gabriel's words troubled Mary, but she chose to embrace her calling to bear the promised seed of redemption. The time had come to undo the deathly damage caused by the curse and to fulfill the messianic promise given that fateful day (Genesis 3:15). God selected a young virgin from the dusty Galilean village of Nazareth, betrothed to the village carpenter. Without hesitation, Mary presented herself as a willing servant to give birth and nurture the Christ-child (Luke 1:38). James notes, "Mary's decision to embrace God's purposes unleashed an avalanche of difficulties and drew her into a disorienting mix of breathtaking privilege and unspeakable pain."[33] Privilege usually carries a costly price tag.

Still, the stylized images of the holy family imprinted on millions of Christmas cards cannot capture the social and cultural dynamics at work in this narrative. As an unwed teenager, Mary's pregnancy placed her in a risky situation, and her far-fetched tale of angelic visitation most likely compounded the problem. In a patriarchal honor/shame society, Mary faced the possibility of death, divorce, or expulsion as a sinful outcast. Moreover, Mary faced a daunting task explaining the situation to Joseph as her supposed 'indiscretion' constituted betrayal and brought shame on him. That culture considered honor killings as just legal retribution in this type of shameful circumstance to put away evil and to restore a family's honor (Deuteronomy 22:20-21). Therefore, Joseph held the power of life and death over Mary, and her fate rested in his hands.

Nevertheless, Joseph was not just an average man; he was a righteous man (Matthew 1:19). Matthew used the Greek word, *dikaios*, meaning "upright, just, fair, and equitable," as an adjective for Joseph. Carolyn James rightly observes that Joseph played "a strategic and indispensable role in the larger story of redemption."[34] He did not merely fill an 'extra' walk-on part, but Joseph remained key; otherwise, the entire Christological saga collapsed without "this remarkable man."[35] God's decision to use Mary and Joseph for His redemptive purpose was predicated as much on Joseph's judicious righteousness and strong moral character as on Mary's faithful trust and willing courage. Joseph's stalwart righteousness and steadfast support of Mary remained absolutely vital for the successful fulfillment of their messianic assignment.

Reading the Scripture through a Western lens causes many to gloss over the harsh reality of Mary and Joseph's situation or even grasp how they felt or what they faced. In their first-century collectivist culture, honor and shame represented reciprocal moral values that integrated the individual into the group and reflected conferred public esteem in conjunction with a person's sensitivity to public opinion.[36] Since ascribed honor came from the group, Mary's pregnancy placed Joseph under severe public pressure, and marriage would have been out of the question. Many would have seen Joseph's decision to divorce Mary privately as a sign of masculine weakness. Nevertheless, he emerges from the pages of Scripture as a mighty man who lived the message of seeking God's kingdom first and putting the needs of Mary above his own.

Instead of demanding a divorce or putting her to death, Joseph took Mary as his wife after God sent an angel to reveal the truth about her pregnancy. Joseph essentially chose to join in Mary's 'shame' instead of defending his honor.[37] A "remarkably godly, selfless, and courageous" woman, Mary met her match in Joseph.[38] Together, Joseph and Mary represent God's A-team and provide one of the best biblical examples of His blessed male/female alliance. Carolyn James enjoins, "Christians would do well to reflect on the selfless way this man and woman worked together to advance God's cause."[39]

Acceptance of her redemptive mission essentially lit a match that caused her entire life to go up in smoke. Nevertheless, she willingly answered the call to lay down her life, her dreams, and her plans for the advancement of God's missional purposes, and Joseph walked beside her every step of the way. Moreover, he spent the remainder of his life ensuring Mary's success in fulfilling her divine mission. James elaborates, "He served as midwife at the birth of Jesus and adopted Mary's child as his own."[40] When the angel warned him of Herod's murderous plot, Joseph even shut down his business and relocated to a different country to protect Mary and Jesus.[41]

Going against the tide of cultural norms, Joseph "denied himself in a hundred ways"; thus, he embodies "the ideal sort of husband" who sacrificially loves his wife and gives himself for her in the manner described in Ephesians 5:25.[42] James further notes, "Joseph was a man ahead of his time. He came alongside Mary and adapted himself to his wife. According to human convention, this was all backwards. But Joseph was a disciple too."[43] He needed Mary to be successful because their salvation and the salvation of the world depended upon the accomplishment of her assignment.

Indeed, God mobilized Mary and Joseph to participate in His redemptive rescue mission to seek and save the lost; moreover, their missional marriage blessed the world.[44] James wisely remarks, "Their focus wasn't on roles or rules, cultural expectations, or power and authority. They focused solely on what God was calling *each* of them to do, and together they embraced God's mind-boggling purposes."[45] In mutual submission to God's call, they laid down their lives and joined forces to bring forth life, to bring forth redemption, to bring forth Jesus, *the true face of submission.*

In a diametrically different manner, Jesus Himself truly defines biblical submission. Submission represents an attribute of Jesus, not "a negative obligation on women but the natural outworking of the gospel in every Christian's life. We were created to be like Jesus, and we cannot be like him if we leave out submission."[46] New Testament writers always spoke of Jesus when addressing this topic because His version of submission was "thoughtful, strong, purposeful, and sacrificial."[47] Carolyn James calls to our attention that the standard Jesus presented was not "about *giving in* to the whims and wishes of others. The submission Jesus models is gospel centered, for he was aligning himself with God's purposes and pouring himself out to rescue a lost humanity (Philippians 2:3-9)."[48]

Christ's kind of submission involves *giving out* and encapsulates the gospel in action. Jesus came to restore God's Creation vision for His image bearers, not make minor adjustments to a broken relational system rooted in humanity's fall. Thus, reducing submission to a tiebreaking decision or an excuse for female domination trivializes this Christian attribute.

Submission represents a divine "power tool for changing lives, renovating the planet and putting our world to rights from the inside out" as believers "pour out their lives for others."[49]

Submission embodies strength, not weakness. Submission brings freedom from selfishness, thereby enabling you to esteem others and to look out for their best interests with love. It repairs human brokenness, resulting in liberty from the law of sin and death. Indeed, men and women who model Jesus' brand of loving, sacrificial submission radiate His grace and become His face—*the true face of submission.*

Chapter Five Footnotes:

1. Norris, "Anthropology," Class lecture notes, Systematic Theology.

2. Ibid.

3. Harvey, *Imago Dei*, 25.

4. James, *Lost Women*, 30.

5. James, *Half the Church*, 158.

6. Carolyn Custis James, *The Gospel of Ruth: Loving God Enough to Break the Rules* (Grand Rapids, MI: Zondervan, 2008), 158.

7. Ibid.

8. Ibid.

9. Ibid., 159.

10. Ibid., 158.

11. Ibid., 159.

12. Ibid.

13. Stephen P. Beck, "Submission," sermonillustrations.com http://www.sermonillustrations.com/a-z/s/ submission.htm

14. D. A. Carson, "I Peter," in *Commentary on the New Testament Use of the Old Testament*, eds. G. K. Beale and D. A. Carson (Grand Rapids, MI: Baker Academic, 2007), 1043.

15. Ibid.

16. Craig Keener, *Paul, Women and Wives: Marriage and Women's Ministry in the Letters of Paul* (Grand Rapids: Baker Academic, eBook edition created 2012), Loc. 2795.

17. Christopher Perry, "Family, Gender Roles, and Marriage in the Ancient Near East and Greco-Roman World," December 2016, 10.

18. Keener, *The IVP Bible Background Commentary*, 551.

19. Keener, *Paul, Women and Wives*, Loc. 2749.

20. Ibid., Loc. 2783, 2733.

21. Perry, "Family, Gender Roles, and Marriage," 45.

22. Ibid.

23. Clinton E. Arnold, *Ephesians – Exegetical Commentary on the New Testament* (Grand Rapids, MI: Zondervan, 2010), 383.

24. Keener, *Paul, Women and Wives*, Loc. 2745.

25. Ibid., Loc. 2749.

26. Ibid., Loc. 2745.

27. Ibid., Loc. 2761.

28. Ibid., Loc. 2770.

29. Ibid.

30. Ibid., Loc. 2775.

31. James, *Lost Women*, 165.

32. Ibid., 166.

33. Ibid., 165.

34. Carolyn Custis James, *Malestrom: Manhood Swept into the Currents of a Changing World* (Grand Rapids: Zondervan, 2015), 159.

35. Ibid.

36. David D. Gilmore, ed., "Introduction: The Shame of Dishonor," in *Honor and Shame and the Unity of the Mediterranean* (Washington, DC: American Anthropological Association, 1987), 3.

37. James, *Malestrom*, 167.

38. James, *Lost Women*, 173.

39. Ibid.

40. Ibid.

41. Ibid.

42. Ibid.

43. Ibid.

44. James, *Malestrom*, 171.

45. Ibid., italics original.

46. James, *The Gospel of Ruth*, 161, 168.

47. Ibid., 161.

48. James, *Half the Church*, 121, italics original.

49. James, *The Gospel of Ruth*, 168.

A Wall or a Door

Dress is a trifling matter, but it gives also the outward sign from which people in general can, and often do, judge upon the inward state of mind and feeling of a person.

—Queen Victoria

History stands in mute testimony to the destructive results of immodesty. Evil does not encroach overnight. Instead, like the descending rays of the sun, darkness creeps in unawares on silent feet. As discussed in previous chapters, it takes only one small bite of poisonous fruit to initiate the gradual process of desensitization and to usher in the acceptance of formerly prohibited practices. Seemingly with no jolt of conscience, standards of decency decreased with each succeeding decade. Things considered unthinkable in the '50s and '60s or even the '70s, '80s, and '90s are now commonplace in the twenty-first century. Removing boundaries to certain behaviors opened the door to escalating immorality with each passing day. Sensual appetites, jaded by the proclivity towards promiscuity, seek for new ways to indulge their perverted lusts. Virtue, modesty, chastity, and innocence became outdated concepts, pushing our culture to slide deeper and deeper into the swamp of sensuality.

The wise man Solomon warned of the menace found on the downward path of degeneration. Of the wanton woman attired like a harlot, he gave this admonition in Proverbs 7:24-27:

Now therefore, listen to me, my children;
Pay attention to the words of my mouth:

Desired By The King

Do not let your heart turn aside to her ways,
Do not stray into her paths;
For she has cast down many wounded,
And all who were slain by her were strong men.
Her house is the way to hell,
Descending to the chambers of death.

Sadly, society, by and large, continues to ignore the wisdom of the prudent philosopher.

Perhaps a journey back to the nineteenth century might serve to illustrate the decline of modesty more fully. While reading *The Country Register*, my mother came across a reprint of an advice column entitled "Abigail's Advice from the 1890s." Abigail Bradshaw, a Victorian lady and advice columnist, answered questions from readers, and the following etiquette excerpt provides an interesting peek into the past:

> *Dear Abigail,*
> *While reading some literature provided to me by a good friend, I came upon a small section of Do's and Don'ts. These were written in reference to proper etiquette, and it was mentioned that a lady should not remove or put on her gloves in the street. There was much discussion between myself and other ladies I associate with about why this might be. I would appreciate it if you would be so kind as to explain why this would be of importance.*
> *Thank you,*
> *Lady Anne*

> *Dear Lady Anne,*
> *Aside from the value of keeping the complexion of the hands pure and unsullied by the damaging rays of the sun, "there is nothing that*

marks the true lady as much as the perfection of neatness in gloves and shoes. To be well gloved and have one's feet neatly clad, no matter how plain the attire, is to be well dressed," as stated in Social Etiquette, 1896. *For a woman to be seen in public putting on her gloves or removing them in the street is certainly indicative of poor breeding. It would be the same as lifting the hem of the skirt and revealing an ankle, heaven forbid! Always keep in mind the following from "The Glory of Woman," 1896: "A lady should be orderly in the smallest matters." How one is dressed reveals one's character.* Social Etiquette *of 1896 elaborates on this reasoning: "The beautiful is the suitable. A woman careless of her dress is either unloved or unhappy. Dress is really a department of manners and appeals to the eye with the same force that gracious words and softly keyed voices appeal to the ear." I trust this will help you and your friends to keep propriety in mind and the gloves buttoned when out of doors.*

> *Yours sincerely,*
> *Abigail Bradshaw*

My, how times changed in just over one hundred years! Wearing gloves and covering ankles went by the wayside, and now full-body exposure depicts the norm. James Atlas rightly observed, "Where the Victorians' sensual longing was veiled, ours is aggressive to the point of violence." Photos of women in extremely abbreviated clothing appear on billboards, fill magazine pages, and glut social media feeds. Even popular gospel artists and other 'Christian' influencers participate in this normalization of nakedness by posting maternity photographs of them and their spouses in abbreviated undergarments and/or sexy lingerie with suggestive captions on their Instagram pages. Fashion commentator, Toby Fischer-Mirkin, writes about the effect of presenting yourself in this manner, "Wearing lingerie as a fashion statement shatters cultural and fashion taboos by allowing others a glimpse of our most intimate self. When worn outside the bedroom, it sends boudoir signals of intimacy" that induces fantasizing by the viewers.[1] Is it appropriate for someone professing to follow Jesus to present herself in this manner? Does it glorify God or focus on the flesh?

The words of Cole Porter certainly sum up the modern mind-set, *In olden days, a glimpse of stocking was looked on as shocking, now heaven knows anything goes.* Considering the downward direction of current trends, it is difficult to fathom a world where modesty walls once shielded women from undue exposure as they descended from their carriages. Walking the streets, even after dark, did not pose much danger to ladies of former generations. According to Tocqueville, "a woman in America could walk anywhere alone without fear, so great was men's respect for their modesty."[2] Holding gentlewomen in high esteem, gentlemen during more genteel times avoided intruding on a woman's space with unwanted attention. Thus, the demure demeanor of the fairer sex afforded them a greater level of courtesy and respect. Wendy Shalit notes that societal support for modesty also provided "a counterweight" that balanced the feminine desire to please thereby "enabling young women to test men's character, in order to choose a suitable partner."[3]

Using humor to depict the ongoing digression of fads and immodest styles, a speaker once stated, "In the past it took an entire sheep to clothe a woman, but now a silkworm can do it on his lunch hour."[4] While you may chuckle at his analogy, the fallout from the designer world created a vacuum of decency in every level of life. During warmer weather, many women walk around semi-naked. Instead of getting dressed for work, they get 'undressed' for work. Women wear undergarments and provocative lingerie for parties, and Victoria's Secret is a popular place to purchase prom dresses (or rather 'un-dresses'). 'Victoria' has no secrets!

An *Indianapolis News* editorial dated October 10, 1995, stated, "Those who minimize the correlation between modest dress and sexual promiscuity deceive themselves and others." Shalit writes, "It is no accident that harassment, stalking, and rape all increased when we decided to let everything hang out. A society that has declared war on embarrassment is one that is hostile to women."[5] Rape continues to rise, including date rape, acquaintance rape, and even classroom rape. Surrounded by peer pressure, young girls give away their virginity, often to random guys they hardly know. Many view chastity as a liability standing in the way of their popularity. Moreover, parents no longer empower their children to say no to sex or teach them the immense value of maintaining their purity. Instead of protecting them, parents rent hotel rooms on prom night so their kids can freely engage in promiscuous sex.

Modern feminists decry the "every woman a lady" ideal as sexism that turned "women into property," but it seems that abandoning this value "made women all the more into property."[6] They told us modesty, "rules, and codes of conduct were sexist, and that's why our mothers got rid of them."[7] Interestingly enough, radical feminist, Camille Paglia, championed normalizing pornography saying, "what is *needed* now…[is] *more* pornography, *better* pornography. Pornography everywhere!"[8] The sanction of modesty, however, gave women the right to say no to unwanted male advances, and a woman's good opinion of a man was revered.

Today's culture of immodesty, on the other hand, disrespects women by telling them to lust like men and to feel comfortable putting their bodies on public display. Now, these same women report feeling "more at the mercy of male desire."[9] Ironically, feminists' efforts to abolish male courtesy and to normalize pornography resulted in greater sexism and the objectification of women.

Advertisers use scantily clad female bodies to sell everything, including houses, cars, boats, alcohol, cigarettes, and phones. Portraits of air-brushed models and Hollywood stars splash across highway billboards and plaster the pages of numerous publications. Women, in their quest to measure up to this enhanced beauty fantasy, spend billions seeking illusionary perfection. Consequently, many suffer from eating disorders and some even resort to cutting and self-mutilation. Exploitation of the female sex flourishes under the guise of fashion, beauty, desirability, and sexual freedom. Trace the money trail, however, and you will discover the true underlying motivation for this manipulative abuse of women's self-image. First Timothy 6:10 unmasks the true nature of this beast, *For the love of money is a root of all kinds of evil.*

English novelist, Anthony Trollope, observed "that modesty is a charm well worth preserving." Unfortunately, the cultural sexual glut causes women to lose their feminine mystique. An old Gaelic proverb reveals the reason for this causal effect, *Modesty is the beauty of women.* The loss of modesty results in a loss of beauty. Have you noticed women are not very beautiful anymore? Just look around. Take a walk through an airport or a shopping mall, and you will be hard pressed to find attractive women. They wear sloppy outfits, Spandex pants and shorts that accentuate the negative, or immodest clothing leaving nothing to the imagination and highlighting every figure flaw. Women lop off their long hair and tint it in unnatural hues, including pink, purple, blue, and green. Tattoos and body piercings mutilate their flesh while they smear hideous colors on their faces, feet, and fingernails. All in the name of beauty—someone's convoluted idea of beauty.

Nevertheless, adopting this cheap imitation of comeliness can have deadly consequences according to an editorial published in *The Observer* on April 7, 2002. An excerpt of the editorial entitled "Makeup kit holds hidden dangers of cancer" reads as follows:

A Wall or a Door

Women are being exposed to deadly diseases through the everyday use of common cosmetics bought over the counter, according to a new study. The growing list of synthetic ingredients manufacturers add to their products are turning the most innocent shampoos and moisturizers into cocktails of toxins that could cause cancer over years of sustained use.

In Drop Dead Gorgeous: Protecting Yourself from the Hidden Dangers of Cosmetics, *authors Kim Erickson and Dr. Samuel S. Epstein reveal how manufacturers exploit loopholes in legislation designed to protect the public.*

"These synthetic ingredients are inexpensive, stable, and have a long shelf life," said Erickson. "Manufacturers love them, but although the majority of products appear safe in the short run, the results from long-term use could be deadly."

The UK cosmetics industry, which employs more than 20,000 people and accounts for 4.5 billion pounds in sales each year, is regulated under the Department of Trade and Industry's 1996 Cosmetic Products (Safety) Regulations.

But while regulations have approved more than 3,000 ingredients for cosmetic use in Europe, Erickson warns that many more find their way into use through loopholes, such as the caveat that allows products to contain traces of banned substances if they could not reasonably be removed during or after manufacture.

"Modern cosmetics contain a host of dubious ingredients, which would be more at home in a test tube than on our faces," said Erickson. "Coal tar colours, phenylenediamine, benzene, even formaldehyde, are just a few of the synthetic chemicals commonly included in shampoos, skin creams, and blushes—toxins which are absorbed into your skin with every use."

Unlike food or drugs, cosmetics and their raw ingredients are not subject to review or independent pre-market approval, a situation criticized by experts including Dr. Jean Munro, medical director of the Breakspear Hospital, Hertfordshire, which specializes in allergies and has seen 8,000 women since opening in 1982—nearly all of whom were found to have sensitivity to cosmetics.

"There is no question that people are being damaged by their cosmetics," Munro said. "How can they not be? So many things are put into cosmetics now that are carcinogenic, and it is allowed because cosmetics are not considered to be as serious as drugs or food."

Munro believes the presence of large numbers of even small amounts of banned substances means that, over time, users will have been exposed to danger.

"One of the most extreme cases I have seen was a woman whose bone marrow was affected by the chemicals used in hair dye. The level of her blood platelets dropped and she broke out in a severe rash," she said. "The situation as it is plainly dangerous—unacceptably so."

Denise Santamarina, a 34-year-old beautician, has spent 10 years battling chemically induced lupus. "I started getting sick when I began taking cosmetology classes," she said. "Over the next 10 years I suffered from a string of digestive problems, sinus infections and excruciating pain in my back, rib cage and arms. There were days when I would crawl across the floor in pain."

Santamarina was given a chemical screening by doctors which showed high levels of benzene and toluene C, both common ingredients in nail polish and polish remover. After leaving her job and removing all synthetic cosmetics from her dressing table, Santamarina gradually began to recover.

"I am basically better now, but it was a long road to travel," she said. "I still find it hard to believe that I was poisoned by cosmetics, but the cause and effect leave no room for argument."

Erickson believes the adverse effects of toxins are compounded over decades, confusing hormone receptors and slowly altering cell structure. Chemicals are transmitted into the bloodstream in a number of ways: powders have the least absorption, while oily solutions or those designed to increase moisture allow more of the chemical to be absorbed. Eye makeup can be absorbed by the highly sensitive mucous membranes. Lipstick is often chewed off and swallowed.

The United Nations Environmental Program estimates that approximately 70,000 chemicals are in common use across the world with 1,000 new chemicals being introduced every year. Of all the chemicals used in cosmetics, the National Institute of Occupational Safety and Health has reported that nearly 900 are toxic—although other groups attack that figure as being far too conservative.

"Compared to the toxins found in our air, soil, and waterways, cosmetics seem a trivial pursuit to many environmental health and consumer advocacy groups," said Erickson. "But many of the same poisons that pollute our environment, from dioxins to petrochemicals, can be found in the jars and bottles that line our bathroom shelves. Many of these ingredients have been found to cause cancer in laboratory animals," she said. "At best, a visit to your neighborhood cosmetic counter could result in allergies, irritations, and sensitivities."

Stacy Malkan confirms these findings in her book, *Not Just a Pretty Face: The Ugly Side of Beauty*. According to a 2004 study, random umbilical cord blood samples drawn from babies born in US hospitals in August and September of 2004 revealed an astonishing number of chemical pollutants.[10] Malkan avers, "Researchers detected a total of 287 chemicals in the babies' cord blood, including 180 chemicals that cause cancer in humans or animals, 217 that are toxic to the brain and nervous system, and 208 that cause birth defects or abnormal development in animal studies."[11] Malkan meticulously details how the transmission of these contaminants transpires through the expectant mother's use of popular cosmetic items such as lipstick, mascara, nail polish, and more. She writes, "Most chemicals in cosmetics have not been tested for their potential to cause long-term health problems such as cancer or reproductive harm."[12] Use of industrial chemicals in consumer products remains largely unregulated in the United States. Yet cosmetic companies sell "hundreds of tons of chemical-containing beauty products every day" and people apply these toxic substances to their bodies.[13]

According to a CDC study of toxic chemicals present in average Americans, scientists "found seven different types of phthalates—a set of industrial chemicals linked to birth defects in the male reproductive system—in 289 people tested. Every single person had dibutyl phthalate (DBP), the most toxic of the phthalates, in his or her body. The ubiquity of phthalates in the general population surprised the scientists."[14] Women of child-bearing age, age twenty to forty, appeared to have the highest levels of DBP, "a chemical that causes birth defects and lifelong reproductive problems in male animals exposed in the womb."[15] Earl Gray, a top phthalate researcher at the US Environmental Protection Agency, said "phthalates disrupt the production of testosterone critical for the masculinization of the male species."[16] This spectrum of adverse health defects "is so common in lab animals exposed to phthalates that scientists termed it 'phthalates syndrome.' "[17]

After extensive, painstaking research, a *Not Too Pretty* report found the majority of beauty products contained phthalates (THA-lates), including popular brands such as Cover Girl, L'Oréal, and Revlon.[18] Christian Dior's aptly named perfume, Poison, the worst offender, "contained four different types of phthalates."[19] Yet none of the products listed "phthalates" on their labels. Taking advantage of major loopholes in federal law allows "the $20-billion-a-year cosmetics industry to put unlimited amounts of phthalates into many personal care products with no required testing, no required monitoring of health effects, and no required labeling."[20] In addition to phthalates, numerous products contain other dangerous contaminants.

Malkan's book contains a plethora of valuable information on this topic, but suffice it to say, adhering to popular fashionable practices can put the health of women and their families at risk. Moreover, given the increase in violence against women, wearing lewd clothing can also put them in a position to experience uncomfortable, even dangerous male aggression. We tend to avoid discussing the correlation between immodest dress and sexual harassment, fearing "such a discussion will end up blaming the victim of the harassment."[21] Yet many women report getting unwanted male attention when dressed in a provocative manner. Fashion commentator Toby Fischer-Milkin explains, "Many men perceive sexy clothes as concrete evidence of promiscuity."[22]

Designer Isaac Mizrahi points to another problem caused by female immodesty, *When a woman tries to be alluring to men, it is inevitable that she is going to annoy other women.* Fischer-Milkin writes, "Women tend to view other women who wear revealing clothing as inconsiderate, insincere, and generally less likable than those who dress conservatively."[23] She offers the following example:

Two women walk into a dinner party. The first wears a beige cashmere sweater dress with a shawl wrapped around her shoulders, the other a black velvet micro minidress with a deeply scalloped back that reveals derriere cleavage and a tight bodice emphasizing her ample bosom. Anyone whose eyes fell upon the second woman focused on either her chest or the nakedness of her back.

Those looking at the first woman tend to see her face first and her outfit as part of her overall appearance. As the evening progresses, the seductively dressed woman begins to feel quite uncomfortable, as much because of the cold reception she receives from the other women in the room as from the overly solicitous attention of the men. By contrast, the woman in the beige cashmere sweater dress is approached warmly by male and female guests alike, which makes her feel more relaxed and open.

As they leave the gathering, one guest asks his wife if she was offended by the male attention showered on the woman in the black micromini. The wife responds that she felt embarrassed to see a woman so hungry for attention. Her reaction is not uncommon. Many women feel that an overtly sexual image demeans not only the wearer but all women, because such a look plays into the long-held stereotypes of woman as either whore or Madonna.[24]

Will women ever wake up and realize fashion designers have certain agendas in mind when creating clothing? When questioned about his "Gender Bender" designs, leading fashion designer, Calvin Klein, boldly replied, "These things are seriously thought out."[25] As they design clothes that blur gender lines, destroy female modesty, and sexually exploit women and girls, the walls of moral decency fall one brick at a time. The statement of Publius Cornelius Tacitus rings true, *When a woman has lost her chastity, she will shrink from nothing.*

For all the liberated choices available nowadays to women, it seems they really have not profited from many of these changes. Wendy Shalit proposes the besetting woes of modern young women such as "sexual harassment, stalking, rap, even 'whirlpooling' (when a group of guys surround a girl who is swimming, and then sexually assault her)" represent "expressions of a society which has lost its respect for female modesty."[26] Indeed, divorce rates continue to rise, deadbeat dads abandon their families, and men refuse to marry women, so they opt for non-committed, live-in relationships. Lonely women seeking warmth and companionship engage in casual sex only to be replaced by the next desirable body that comes along. Why? Perhaps immodesty and sexually liberated lifestyles destroyed the place of respect and honor once occupied by modestly chaste ladies.

Unfortunately, immodesty along with looser morals also infiltrated most Christian church denominations. At one time, these churches stood staunchly against many modern amoral practices, but now they consider such a stance antiquated and out of touch. Their preachers even ridicule people who espouse the doctrine of separation and label them as 'legalists.' The following illustration from LaJoyce Martin's book, *Coriander Seed and Honey*, highlights this unfortunate moral deterioration:

> *A century old, the stately old church building in Dallas was eaten away with the cancer of time and erosion. It was a denominational church founded with the name New Hope. My husband was removing the priceless old front doors. These notes, dated prior to 1899, were found: "Scores of members were excluded from the church for the following reasons: dancing, being drunk, suing a fellow member in civil court, going to the show, swearing, swindling, domestic troubles, refusing to pay back church dues, and being the leader of a baseball league." New Hope's history shows that not only do buildings deteriorate over the years, but so values do, also.*

To be clear, I am not advocating for the exclusion of people who make mistakes and need a Savior. Jesus came to seek and to save the lost. This story simply illustrates how value systems gradually deteriorate over time. In my personal archives, I have a gospel tract put out several years ago by the Lutheran church concerning the evils of makeup. Entitled *The Painted Face*, the pamphlet speaks of the biblical references to "painting" in conjunction with ungodliness and immorality. Identifying "painting" as a "mark of the World," it documents its connection with heathenish practices and harlotry. Finally, the writer declares, "Painting hinders our witness and leads to compromise." What a prescient declaration in light of their current stance on this subject and other moral issues of the day!

A public official whose name has been forgotten in the annals of time once declared, *The strength of a nation hinges on the character and modesty of its women.* Many people consider female modesty an idea not deserving of consideration, a taboo subject, or a locked door. Wendy Shalit observes, "Perhaps it seems threatening because it doesn't just ask the question, 'what kind of women do we want to become?'—it provides a very specific answer. And maybe, just maybe, modesty is the answer which could, with all due modesty, flip everything around."[27]

Alice von Hildebrand wisely noted, *God has confined the sexual sphere especially to women, and so, in our age of sexual depravity it is a particular burden which falls on the shoulders of women to foster modesty and to protect the virtue of purity.* Respect for others combined with reverence and love for God should inspire everyone to cultivate a lifestyle of purity by presenting herself in a manner pleasing to the Lord. An item for sale is usually put on display, so if my body is not for sale, why would I display it? Moreover, I am my brother's keeper; thus, I should present myself in a modest manner that does not cause anyone to stumble by inciting lust and heart adultery.

Amongst the orthodox Jews, there is a saying, *ein b'not yisrael hefker*, meaning "the daughters of Israel are not available for public use."[28] What a powerful concept! Sexual modesty declares to the world, "I think *I'm* worth waiting for and worth concealing"; thus, modesty paradoxically denotes self-worth so "you don't need to boast or put your body on display for all to see."[29] Ironically, many equate modesty in dress with having sexual hang-ups, but it "actually permits women precisely not to be hung up about sex."[30] Furthermore, it allows women to be taken seriously without acting like a man or desperately trying to prove their worth by flaunting their flesh. Modesty inherently enhances a woman's intrinsic value.

A Wall or a Door

The University of Missouri conducted an interesting study regarding sexually explicit styles, and the results are enlightening. They asked twenty men and women to "rate the attractiveness of the same woman dressed in both provocative and nonprovocative outfits. Surprisingly, when shown photos of the deliberately provocative outfits, men *did not perceive an increase* in the woman's attractiveness, and women perceived a *decrease* in attractiveness."[31] Fischer-Milkin remarks, "When it comes to sexually explicit styles, it seems both men and women respond most favorably to looks that represent some degree of moderation—old-fashioned as that may sound."[32]

In her excellent book, *Modesty: A New Look at an Old Word*, Marjorie Kinnee outlines some Jewish guidelines for Modesty. The following excerpt taken from chapter ten entitled "Sleeve-Lengths, Hemlines & Such, *tznu 'im* in dress," offers some excellent guidance.

Care for modesty is required in all the following:

◆ *In the manner in which one walks*

◆ *When descending or climbing stairs*

◆ *When sitting or standing on any sort of elevated platform or balcony*

◆ *When sitting very low or crouching*

◆ *When sitting in general*

◆ *When emerging from or getting into a car, bus, etc.*

◆ *When exercising*

◆ *When riding a bike*

Desired By The King

A woman (or girl) first has responsibility for modest dress because the Lord commands it, but she also has a responsibility not to put a stumbling block before others. The commandment is not to dress in a way that would incite lustful thoughts. Rabbinical teaching maintains that this is a responsibility and an obligation that belongs to women and girls. They include the complete torso, the upper arms, and the upper legs in what must be covered. It is considered a form of harlotry to wear items of clothing which alternately conceal and reveal parts of the body which should be hidden.

◆ A face that projects purity is beautiful. (A modest rule of thumb—the focal point of a modestly attired woman should be her face, not her body.)

◆ The view of anyone standing above and to the side of a seated woman should be taken into consideration when evaluating the modesty of a neckline.

◆ Slacks or trousers are forbidden because not only do they reveal the general outline of the upper legs, but they also exhibit and emphasize their entire shape. (Some skintight pants also improperly emphasize one's private parts.) The rabbis say that a woman appearing in public wearing slacks during the time of the Sanhedrin would have been brought before the council and stoned for gross indecency.

◆ Slits that extend above the knee are particularly objectionable for the following reasons:

  • A slit attracts attention because it alternately reveals and conceals the wearer's legs
  • Revealing the upper parts of the legs creates an extreme incitement to lust.

- *The clothing designers' intent is to provoke interest through tantalizing glimpses which invites the gaze to linger. (A* People's Magazine *article concurs, "It's sexier to see a slit up the leg than it is to see the whole bod.")*

◆ *For a woman to respond, saying, "Don't look!" and "Mind your own business!" is brazen. Furthermore, this kind of answer doesn't deal with the problem. A man should be able to go about his business without having to deal with unwanted provocation.*[33]

These teachings offer excellent advice, and careful consideration of their wisdom will benefit both men and women.

Three times in the Song of Solomon, the bride gave a solemn charge,

> **I charge you, O daughters of Jerusalem,**
> **By the gazelles or by the does of the field,**
> **Do not stir up nor awaken love**
> **Until it pleases.**[34]

Enjoining the women, she instructed them not to awaken latent passions outside the bonds of matrimony. Apart from marriage, appropriate restraint should be maintained during one's interactions with the opposite sex.

The groom defined his beloved (Song of Solomon 4:12):

> **A garden enclosed**
> **Is my sister, my spouse,**
> **A spring shut up,**
> **A fountain sealed.**

Notice he identified his beloved as his *sister*, implying a deep level of respect and virtue within their prenuptial relationship.

In the same vein, Paul instructed Timothy in I Timothy 5:2 to treat older women as mothers and younger women as sisters, with all purity. Wendy Shalit points out that a man of honor respects "every female's modesty" whether she is "rich or poor, from the country, or the inner city."[35]

The bridegroom used imagery of a walled garden and a sealed fountain, symbolic of the bride's chastity and devotion to the man of her dreams. This world would be far safer and saner if women returned to this sort of demure demeanor. "The abundance and provision of the garden are metaphoric of the richness and value the two lovers find in each other. The enclosed nature of the garden of love captures the seclusion, privacy, intimacy, and security that the lovers feel in their love."[36] Overtones of Eden permeate the Song's artful language and metaphoric descriptions. Using poetic imagery and expressive emotion, Solomon's Song "preserves a level of mystery that appeals to the whole person" and envisions the Creator's original relational ideal for His image bearers.[37]

Continuing the metaphor in Song of Solomon 8:10, the bride responded, *I am a wall, and my breasts like towers: then was I in his eyes as one that found favour* (KJV). Comparing herself to a garrisoned fortification, she enclosed her feminine attributes behind a bulwark of propriety. Diligence to maintain her maidenly virtue brought favor and respect in the eyes of the king. An upright, godly man cherishes this kind of woman. Contrary to popular culture that advocates immodesty to enhance one's attraction, a woman becomes more alluring when she encircles herself with virtuous conduct and clothing.

In conclusion, let us consider some ways to assess actions and attire. Is there a simple standard you can use for determining whether a garment is modest, one that can be transmitted to your family? How can principles of modesty become a way of life for you and your children?

Song of Solomon 8:8-9 provides a clear, concise answer to these questions,

A Wall or a Door

We have a little sister,
And she has no breasts.
What shall we do for our sister
In the day when she is spoken for?
If she is a wall,
We will build upon her
A battlement of silver;
And if she is a door,
We will enclose her
With boards of cedar.

Employing an allegorical approach, the writer acquainted us with *a little sister* that *has no breasts*. Characterizing a pre-pubescent girl, these verses speak of the family's looking ahead to her betrothal. Pondering the importance of instilling proper behavioral patterns within this little lass during her formative years, they used the same metaphor found in verse 10. If she was a fortified *wall*, indicative of protected moral purity, she would be honored with a valuable dowry of silver.

On the other hand, if this maiden was a *door*, action must be taken. The New Living Translation provides greater clarity on this part of the verse, *But if she is promiscuous, like a swinging door, we will block her door with a cedar bar.* Her family must intervene and stop the penchant for promiscuity by ingraining a different set of chaste principles within the child. The passage of Scripture illustrates the importance of instilling godly character from an early age. Like Timothy, our children should know the Holy Scriptures which are able to impart wisdom and salvation through faith in Christ Jesus. It is never too early to implant a moral code of conduct within their hearts. Once the wall of modesty gets broken down, it is difficult to repair the breach. Have you noticed how children's fashions are designed to sexualize them at an early age and destroy their God-given inhibitions? There is nothing innocent or unaware in this agenda—it is part of a precise, deadly plan perpetrated by perverse people to groom children immorally by preying upon them and destroying their innocence. Little girls, made up and dressed like prostitutes, are paraded in beauty pageants while little boys dance and prance in drag queen shows. The lethal repercussions from these distorted practices include pedophilia, child pornography, gender dysphoria, abuse, molestation, incest, and even death. We need to wake up and stop the enemy from perpetrating his evil agenda on our children.

In addition to illustrating youthful modesty or the lack thereof, the two analogies of a *wall* or a *door* provide a biblical measuring device for your clothing. A *wall* is a continuous structure forming a rampart. Built for defensive purposes, it encloses, surrounds, and separates one from dangerous trespassers or enemies. Conversely, a *door* represents an entryway or passage that provides a means of access.

When assessing an outfit, ask yourself the following questions. Does this dress project the concept of a fortified *wall*, or like a *door*, does it provide outside access to my body? Are my feminine attributes protected and concealed from roving eyes, or are they openly displayed like items for sale? Would this garment nourish the spirit of holiness or promote lustful thoughts in others or even myself? Does it reveal my undergarments or too much skin? Typical of a *door*, does my clothing amplify sensuality, or does it enhance the beauty of holiness? If I wear this outfit, will I be a **wall** or a **door**?

Chapter Six Footnotes:

1. Toby Fischer-Mirkin, *Dress Code: Understanding the Hidden Meanings of Women's Clothes* (New York, NY: Clarkson Potter Publishers, 1995), 64-65.

2. Wendy Shalit, *A Return to Modesty: Discovering the Lost Virtue* (New York, NY: Simon & Schuster, 1999), 46.

3. Ibid., 56.

4. Jennifer J. Lamp, *His Chosen Bride: Living Out Your Position as Daughter of the King and Bride of Christ* (Wichita, KS: GraceWorks Ministry Press, 1999), 201.

5. Shalit, *A Return to Modesty*, 39.

6. Ibid., 46.

7. Ibid., 47.

8. Ibid., 53.

9. Ibid., 60.

10. Stacy Malkan, *Not Just a Pretty Face: The Ugly Side of Beauty* (Gabriola Island, BC, Canada: New Society Publishers, 2007), 1.

11. Ibid.

12. Ibid., 11.

13. Ibid.

14. Ibid., 15.

15. Ibid.

16. Ibid., 17.

17. Ibid.

18. Ibid., 23.

19. Ibid.

20. Ibid., 24.

21. Shalit, *A Return to Modesty*, 69.

22. Fischer-Mirkin, *Dress Code*, 68.

23. Ibid.

24. Ibid, pp. 68-69.

25. Kidwell and Steele, *Men and Women*, 56.

26. Shalit, *A Return to Modesty*, 10.

27. Ibid., 80.

28. Ibid., 131.

29. Ibid., 132.

30. Ibid., 72.

31. Fischer-Mirkin, *Dress Code*, 69.

32. Ibid., 70.

33. Marjorie Kinnee, *Modesty: A New Look at an Old Word* (Rochester, MI: Bro-Kin Publishing, 2001), pp. 96-98.

34. Song of Solomon 2:7; 3:5; 8:4.

35. Shalit, *A Return to Modesty*, 149.

36. Ryken, Wilhoit, and Longman, eds., *Dictionary of Biblical Imagery*, 317.

37. Ibid., 806.

Desired by the King

What we love we grow to resemble.

—Bernard of Clairvaux

The original idea for this book came during a ladies' conference in the spring of 2001. As the speaker ministered from Psalm 45, the Lord whispered softly to my spirit these words, *Desired by the King.* This book juxtaposes the enemy's evil agenda against God's perfect plan. The first three chapters of this book unmask the enemy's war on women. He markets his evil agenda using appealing rhetoric such as feminism, women's liberation, pro-choice, and sexual freedom. The father of lies uses the same tactic over and over. He wraps his deadly package in cunning deception, making evil appear good and good appear evil. Projecting his wicked attributes on God, satan convinces humanity that God wants the worst for His image bearers. Then the trickster offers the same old solution—just take a bite of this forbidden fruit to improve on the Creator's plan for you. But the opposite always happens—the seed of rebellion produces a bitter harvest of destruction and death.

The next three chapters return us to the basics of God's perfect plan and offer the antidote for the enemy's poisoned fruit. A meek and quiet spirit remains priceless and provides divine protection. Modesty and purity increase a woman's value and allure. Mutual submission, sacrificial love, unselfishness, and respect represent God's relational plan for His image bearers. Thus, society thrives when men and women support one another and celebrate their God-given differences. To be a man is good and to be a woman is good! Together we image God and present a redemptive picture of Christ and His church.

God's plan brings forth life while the enemy's agenda creates a culture of death. God transforms humanity while satan deforms humanity. Psalm 149:4 declares, *For the LORD takes pleasure in His people; He will beautify the humble* [meek] *with salvation.* God takes pleasure in His people, making their lives more beautiful, while the devil walks around like a roaring lion, seeking to devour God's image bearers. God is the giver of every good and perfect gift. God gives power, love, and soundness of mind because He is love and His love is perfected in us as we follow Him. Satan foments fear because it breeds torment, and this treacherous thief steals, kills, and destroys everything he touches. The enemy's earthly, sensual, demonic wisdom breeds hatred, bitter envy, jealousy, strife, selfishness, and confusion, causing those who follow his perverse path to experience disorder and evil of every kind. His *trans*-agenda produces chaos and deathly devastation. Indeed, Jesus called the devil a murderer in John 8:44, *He was a murderer from the beginning, and does not stand in the truth, because there is no truth in him. When he speaks a lie, he speaks from his own resources, for he is a liar and the father of it.*

Proverbs 4:19 describes the way of the wicked as total darkness, and satan's broad way descends into an eternal abyss filled with wailing and gnashing of teeth. But God calls us out of darkness into His marvelous light, and the way of the righteous resembles a shining light that shines ever brighter unto the perfect day as we are *trans*formed into His image from glory to glory. First John 3:2 describes the culmination of this *trans*-formational process, *Beloved, now we are children of God; and it has not yet been revealed what we shall be, but we know that when He is revealed, we shall be like Him, for we shall see Him as He is.* We shall be like Him!

Psalm 45, the inspiration for this book's title, paints a beautiful picture of that perfect day when we see Jesus face to face. It depicts the celebration of the ages when the King of kings and His bride unite for all eternity. Set against the backdrop of an Oriental imperial wedding, this royal psalm embodies the very essence of Christ and the church. Lee Roy Martin, Professor of Old Testament and Biblical Languages, comments, "Any Psalm that mentions the king is automatically connected to Jesus Christ and Psalm 45 is no exception. Beyond the common allegorical concept of Messianic Psalms, however, Psalm 45 6-7 has the further distinction of being cited in the New Testament (Heb. 1:8-9) where it is interpreted as a reference to Jesus. It follows that if the 'king' signifies Jesus then the 'queen' must signify the Church, the Bride of Christ."[1]

The composer set this messianic psalm, addressed to the chief musician, to "The Lilies." The Septuagint translates the superscription, "Set to The Lilies," as *huper tōn alloiōthēsomeōn*, meaning "for those who will be changed."[2] This Greek translation connotes an underlying idea linking *lilies* and *the seasonal transformation* symbolic of imagery tied to "Passover, new creation, and resurrection, for which lilies are an ancient symbol."[3] The superscription further identifies it as "a song of loves" exemplifying the wedding theme and its function as a wedding song for the marriage of a royal couple.[4]

After the superscription, the composer began with this ecstatic exclamation,

> *My heart is overflowing with a good theme;*
> *I recite my composition concerning the King;*
> *My tongue is the pen of a ready* [skillful] *writer.*

Daniel Segraves writes, "The words translated 'a good theme' (*dabar tov*) mean literally 'a good word.' "[5] Given its messianic context, "a good word" could be read as referring to the gospel which means "good news." Segraves adds that Hebrews, the book connecting Psalm 45 with the Messiah, "identifies New Testament believers as those who have 'tasted the good word of

God' (Hebrews 6:5). Since the theme of Psalm 45 is 'the King' (verse 1), and since the King is God (verse 6), it seems reasonable to understand the psalm as a poetic description of events surrounding the proclamation of the gospel message."[6]

According to Middle Eastern custom, the psalm places the bridegroom as the center of attention, and truly, at the great day, God will be all in all! Following this tradition throughout the beginning stanzas, the psalmist exuberantly extolled the grace and glory of the triumphant warrior King. His eulogy portrays a priestly monarch who forever reigns in righteousness.

> *You are fairer than the sons of men;*
> *Grace is poured upon Your lips;*
> *Therefore God has blessed You forever.*
> *Gird Your sword upon Your thigh, O Mighty One,*
> *With Your glory and Your majesty.*
> *And in Your majesty ride prosperously because of truth,*
> *humility, and righteousness;*
> *And Your right hand shall teach You awesome things.*
> *Your arrows are sharp in the heart of the King's enemies;*
> *The peoples fall under You.*
> *Your throne, O God, is forever and ever;*
> *A scepter of righteousness is the scepter of Your kingdom.*
> *You love righteousness and hate wickedness;*
> *Therefore God, Your God, has anointed You*
> *With the oil of gladness more than Your companions.*

Verse 3 lauds the Messiah as the "Mighty One" girded with the sword and graced with glory and majesty. This title correlates with Isaiah 9:6, which identifies Him as the "Mighty God." Moreover, the Messiah portrayed "as a conquering king on a steed" riding prosperously because of "truth, humility, and righteousness" conducts a successful military campaign against his enemies.[7] This imagery parallels Revelation 19:11, *Now I saw heaven opened, and behold, a white horse. And He who*

*sat on him was called Faithful and True, and in righteousness
He judges and makes war.*

The discussion turns to wedding preparations in verse 8,
describing the King's garments and the palace setting for the
marriage celebration.

*All Your garments are scented with myrrh and aloes and cassia,
Out of the ivory palaces, by which they have made You glad.*

Daniel Segraves explains, "The phrase translated, 'out of the
ivory palaces, by which they have made You glad' could be
translated, 'from the luxurious palaces comes the music of
stringed instruments that makes you happy.' "[8]
Verses 9-14 speak of the regal wedding party including
the queen and her attendants.

*Kings' daughters are among Your honorable women;
At Your right hand stands the queen in gold from Ophir.
Listen, O daughter,
Consider and incline your ear;
Forget your own people also, and your father's house;
So the King will greatly desire your beauty;
Because He is your Lord, worship Him.
And the daughter of Tyre will come with a gift;
The rich among the people will seek your favor.
The royal daughter is all glorious within the palace;
Her clothing is woven with gold.
She shall be brought to the King in robes of many colors;
The virgins, her companions who follow her, shall be
brought to You.*

During the marriage of the monarch, the bride and her
attendants add glory to the royal court. Verses 9 and 13 specifically reference the lavishness of the bride's golden attire. As

Segraves expounds, "The queen's adornment included 'gold from Ophir.' Ophir was known as the source of fine gold. In conjunction with its messianic theme," the description of her wedding garments could be compared to Revelation 19:7-8.[9] Lee Roy Martin concurs, "The figure of the queen is expanded comparing the queen's golden garments to the believer's garment which is the 'holiness of Christ.' "[10]

Pausing in verses 10 and 11, the narrator gives advice to the King's betrothed. Like Rebekah of old, she must be willing to forsake all, leaving her own people and her father's house. Nothing must supersede her love for the King. Her renunciation of all others and acknowledgment of His lordship captures His heart, causing Him to desire her beauty. The King is smitten when He beholds His beloved in her lovely wedding attire.

Skillfully creating a word picture, the ballad continues with the details of this spectacular event. Wealthy wedding guests seeking the favor of the noble couple bring rich presents. Daniel Segraves notes the gift from the daughter of Tyre and the pursuit of the "rich among the people" for the bride's favor "evokes prophecies found elsewhere concerning the universal homage" paid to the Messiah "and thus to His royal court."[11]

With gladness and rejoicing they shall be brought;
They shall enter the King's palace.
Instead of Your fathers shall be Your sons,
Whom You shall make princes in all the earth.
I will make Your name to be remembered in all generations;
Therefore the people shall praise You forever and ever.

With great jubilation, the resplendent wedded pair, along with their wedding guests, enter the King's palace for an eternal celebration, ***and so shall we ever be with the Lord.***[12] This grand affair culminates in exaltation throughout all generations.

The invitations have been sent, a place has been prepared, the arrangements are in order, and the King eagerly awaits His imminent marriage. Before long the voice of our beloved Lord will summon His bride to come away with Him.

My beloved spoke, and said to me:
"Rise up, my love, my fair one,
And come away.
For lo, the winter is past,
The rain is over and gone.
The flowers appear on the earth;
The time of singing has come,
And the voice of the turtledove
Is heard in our land.
The fig tree puts forth her green figs,
And the vines with the tender grapes
Give a good smell.
Rise up, my love, my fair one,
And come away!"[13]

Gloriously arrayed within and without, the Bride of Christ prepares herself for the marriage supper of the Lamb. Nothing mars her beauty, no spot, wrinkle, or any such thing; she remains holy and without blemish. *You are all fair, my love, And there is no spot in you.*[14] This fair, spotless bride who is *Desired by the King* will rule and reign with Him forever.

Chapter Seven Footnotes:

1. Lee Roy Martin, *The Spirit of the Psalms: Rhetorical Analysis, Affectivity, and Pentecostal Spirituality* (Cleveland, TN: CPT Press, 2018), 195.

2. Daniel L. Segraves, *The Messiah in the Psalms: Discovering Christ in Unexpected Places* (Hazelwood, MO: WAP Academic, 2007), 281.

3. Ibid.

4. Ibid., 159.

5. Ibid., 161.

6. Ibid.

7. Ibid., 162.

8. Ibid., 164.

9. Ibid., 165.

10. Martin, *The Spirit of the Psalms*, 195.

11. Segraves, *The Messiah in the Psalms*, 165. (See Isaiah 60:3; Zechariah 14:16-17; Revelation 21:24-26).

12. I Thessalonians 4:17, KJV.

13. Song of Solomon 2:10-13.

14. Song of Solomon 4:7.

Reference Bibliography

Arnold, Clinton E. *Ephesians – Exegetical Commentary on the New Testament*. Grand Rapids, MI: Zondervan, 2010.

Arnold, Joshua. "Using 'Wrong' Pronouns Could Lead to Suspensions in Virginia Public Schools." dailysignal.com, 5/16/22. https://www.dailysignal.com/2022/05/16/using-wrong-pronouns-could-lead-to-school-suspensions-in-virginia-public-schools/

Baskerville, Stephen, Ph.D. "Divorce as Revolution." http://www.ejfi.org/family/family-26.htm

Beck Stephen P. "Submission." sermonillustrations.com. http://www.sermonillustrations.com/a-z/s/submission.htm

Bernikow, Louise. *The American Women's Almanac*. New York, NY: Berkley Publishing Group, 1997.

Belleville, Linda L. *Women Leaders and the Church: Three Crucial Questions*. Grand Rapids: Baker Books, 2000.

Bilezikian, Gilbert. *Beyond Sex Roles: What the Bible Says about a Woman's Place in Church and Family, 3rd edition*. Grand Rapids: Baker Academic, 2006.

Boyd, Stephen B. *The Men We Long to Be: Beyond Domination to a New Christian Understanding of Manhood.* New York: HarperCollins, 1995.

Brenner, A. *The Israelite Woman: Social Role and Literary Type in Biblical Narrative.* Biblical Seminar 2; Sheffield: JSOT Press, 1994.

Brueggemann, Walter. *1 and 2 Kings.* Smith and Helwys Bible Commentary; Macon, GA: Smith & Helwys, 2000.

Cahill, Thomas. *The Gifts of the Jews: How a Tribe of Desert Nomads Changed the Way Everyone Thinks and Feels.* New York, NY: Anchor Books, 1998.

Carson, D. A. "I Peter." Pages 1015-1045 in *Commentary on the New Testament Use of the Old Testament.* Edited by G. K. Beale and D. A. Carson. Grand Rapids, MI: Baker Academic, 2007.

DeRouchie, Jason S. "Confronting the Transgender Storm: New Covenant Reflections on Deuteronomy 22:5." *Journal for Biblical Manhood and Womanhood* 21/1 2016: 58-69.

Evans, Sarah B., Ed.D, and Joan P. Avis, Ph.D. *The Women Who Broke all the Rules.* Naperville, IL: Sourcebooks, Inc., 1999.

Evans, Sarah M. *Born for Liberty.* New York: Simon & Schuster, 1989, 1997.

Fischer-Mirkin, Toby. *Dress Code: Understanding the Hidden Meanings of Women's Clothes.* New York, NY: Clarkson Potter Publishers, 1995.

Fox, Megan. "9 Secrets to Keep Your Daughter from Becoming a Slut." pjmedia.com, 3/9/14. https://pjmedia.com/lifestyle/2014/3/9/9-secrets-to-keep-your-daughter-from-becoming-a-slut/

Gaines, Janet Howe. "How Bad Was Jezebel?" biblicalarchaeology.org, 3/22/2. https://www.biblicalarchaeology.org/daily/people-cultures-in-the-bible/people-in-the-bible/how-bad-was-jezebel/

Gilder, George. *Men and Marriage*. Gretna, LA: Pelican, 1986.

Gilligan, Carol. *In a Different Voice*. Cambridge: Harvard University Press, 1993.

Gilmore, David D., ed. "Introduction: The Shame of Dishonor." Pages 2-17 in *Honor and Shame and the Unity of the Mediterranean*. Washington, DC: American Anthropological Association, 1987.

Groningen, Gerard Van. "1-2 Kings." Pages 231-262 in *Evangelical Commentary on the Bible*. Edited by Walter A. Elwell. Grand Rapids: Baker Books, 2001.

Harvey, Ruth. *Imago Dei: Restoring the Creator's DNA*. Akron, OH: 48hrbooks.com, 2019.

Heller, Mikhail. *Cogs in the Wheel*. New York: Knopf, 1988, 168-179, cited in Charles E. Corry, "Evolution of Society," http://www.ejfi.org/Civilization/Civilization-2.htm

Hoffeditz David M. and Gary E. Yates. "Femme Fatale *Redux: Intertextual Connection to Elijah/Jezebel Narratives in Mark 6:14-29*." *Bulletin for Biblical Research* 15/2 2005: 199-221.

Hull, Gretchen Gaebelein. *Equal to Serve: Women and Men Working Together Revealing the Gospel.* Grand Rapids: Baker Books, 1998.

Illustrations on Meekness. bible.org. https://bible.org/node/11449

Ingraham, Christopher. "Less than half of U.S. kids now have a 'traditional' family." washingtonpost.com, 12/23/14. https://www.washingtonpost.com/news/wonk/wp/2014/12/23/less-than-half-of-u-s-kids-now-have-a-traditional-family/

James, Carolyn Custis. *Half the Church: Recapturing God's Global Vision for Women.* Grand Rapids: Zondervan, 2011.

———— *Lost Women of the Bible: The Women We Thought We Knew.* Grand Rapids, MI: Zondervan, 2005.

———— *Malestrom: Manhood Swept into the Currents of a Changing World.* Grand Rapids: Zondervan, 2015.

———— *The Gospel of Ruth: Loving God Enough to Break the Rules.* Grand Rapids, MI: Zondervan, 2008.

Keener, Craig S. *The IVP Bible Background Commentary: New Testament.* Downers Grove, IL: InterVarsity Press, 1993.

———— *Paul, Women and Wives: Marriage and Women's Ministry in the Letters of Paul.* Grand Rapids: Baker Academic, eBook edition created 2012.

Kidwell, Claudia Brush, and Valerie Steele. *Men and Women: Dressing the Part.* Washington: Smithsonian Institute Press, 1989.

Kinnee, Marjorie. *Modesty: A New Look at an Old Word.* Rochester, MI: Bro-Kin Publishing, 2001.

Kupelian, David. *How Evil Works: Understanding and Overcoming the Destructive Forces That Are Transforming America.* New York, NY: Simon & Schuster, 2010.

——*The Marketing of Evil: How Radicals, Elitists, and Pseudo-Experts Sell Us Corruption Disguised as Freedom.* Nashville, TN: Cumberland House Publishers, 2005.

Lamp, Jennifer J. *His Chosen Bride: Living Out Your Position as Daughter of the King and Bride of Christ.* Wichita, KS: GraceWorks Ministry Press, 1999.

Malkan, Stacy. *Not Just a Pretty Face: The Ugly Side of Beauty.* Gabriola Island, BC, Canada: New Society Publishers, 2007.

Martin, Lee Roy. *The Spirit of the Psalms: Rhetorical Analysis, Affectivity, and Pentecostal Spirituality.* Cleveland, TN: CPT Press, 2018.

Moir, Anne, and David Jessel. *Brain Sex: The real difference between Men and Women.* London: Wise Owl Secrets Publishing, 2015 Kindle edition.

Morgan, Robin. *Sisterhood is Powerful.* New York: Random House, 1970.

Norris, David. "Anthropology." Class lecture notes, Systematic Theology, UGST, October 28, 2014.

Packer, J. I., and M. C. Tenney, eds. *Illustrated Manners and Customs of the Bible.* Nashville, TN: Thomas Nelson Publishers, 1980.

Paglia, Camille. "It's a Jungle Out There." *Newsday*, 1991. https://archive.seattletimes.com/archive/?date=199102 17&slug=1266788

Perdue, Leo G., Joseph Blenkinsopp, John J. Collins, and Carol Meyers. *Families in Ancient Israel*. Louisville, KY: Westminster John Knox Press, 1997.

Perry, Christopher. "Family, Gender Roles, and Marriage in the Ancient Near East and Greco-Roman World." December 2016.

Rawlson, Hope. " 'God is Queer,' Duke Divinity Students Proclaim." juicyecumenism.com 4/5/22. https://juicyecumenism.com/2022/04/05/queer-god-duke-divinity/

Renner, Rick. *Sparkling Gems from the Greek: 365 Greek Word Studies for Every Day of the Year To Sharpen Your Understanding of God's Word*. Tulsa, OK: Teach All Nations Printing, 2003.

Richards, Lawrence O. *Complete Bible Handbook*. Waco, TX: Word Books, 1987.

Ryken, Leland, James C. Wilhoit, and Tremper Longman III, eds. *Dictionary of Biblical Imagery: An Encyclopedic Exploration of the Images, Symbols, Motifs, Metaphors, Figures of Speech and Literary Patterns of the* Bible. Downers Grove, IL: IVP Academic, 1998.

Segraves, Daniel L. "Old Testament Law & the New Testament." Class lecture notes, Old Testament Foundations, October 23, 2013.

—— *The Messiah in the Psalms: Discovering Christ in Unexpected Places*. Hazelwood, MO: WAP Academic, 2007.

Shalit, Wendy. *A Return to Modesty: Discovering the Lost Virtue*. New York, NY: Simon & Schuster, 1999.

Smith, Catherine, and Cynthia Greig. *Women in Pants: Manly Maidens, Cowgirls, and Other Renegades*. New York, NY: Harry N. Abrams Publishers, 2003.

Telushkin, Rabbi Joseph. *Biblical Literacy: The Most Important People, Events, and Ideas of the Hebrew Bible*. New York, NY: HarperCollins, 1997.

Unger, Merrill F. *The New Unger's Bible Handbook*. Revised by Gary N. Larson. Chicago, IL: Moody Press, 1984.

Van Meter, Dr. Quentin. "The Terrible Fraud of Transgender Medicine." https://www.youtube.com/watch?v=uC0zn0D_MyM

West, Charlotte. "An unnoticed result of the decline of men in college: It's harder for women to get in." hechingerreport.org, 10/27/21. https://hechingerreport.org/an-unnoticed-result-of-the-decline-of-men-in-college-its-harder-for-women-to-get-in/